STEEPED IN TRADITION

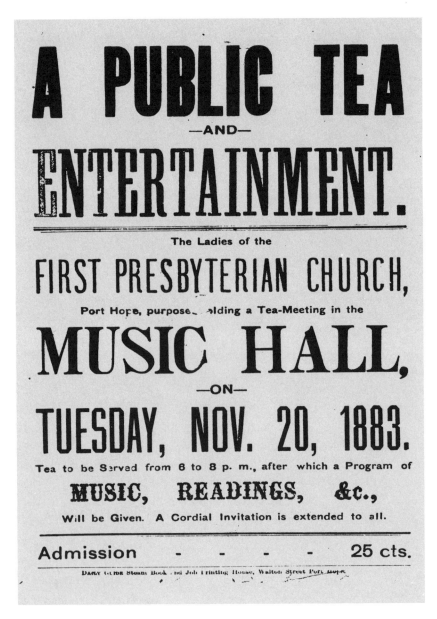

Steeped in Tradition

A Celebration of Tea

Frances Hoffman

Natural Heritage/Natural History Inc.

Published by Natural Heritage/Natural History Inc.
P.O. Box 95, Station O, Toronto, Ontario M4A 2M8

First Edition

Canadian Cataloguing in Publication Data

Hoffman, Frances
  Steeped in tradition: a celebration of tea

Includes index

ISBN 1-896219-18-7

I. Tea 2. Afternoon teas. 3. Tea–Ontario. 4, Tea rooms–Ontario. I. Title.

GT2905. H63 1997 394.1'.5 C97-930193-9

Cover and text design by Norton Hamill Design
Cover photo by George McDermott of author Frances Hoffman at Langdon Hall
Frontispiece photo of an admittance card to attend a community "Public Tea."
Archives of Ontario

Natural Heritage/Natural History Inc. acknowledges the support received for its publishing program from the Canada Council Block Grant Program. We also acknowledge with gratitude the assistance of the Association for the Export of Canadian Books, Ottawa, and the Office of the Ontario Arts Council, Toronto.

PRINTED AND BOUND IN CANADA BY HIGNELL PRINTING, WINNIPEG, MANITOBA

For my dear friend and cousin, Judith Noble

Acknowledgments

For generously sharing their special recipes I am grateful to: Executive Chef Herbert Baur and Manager Carol Muscato of the Queenston Heights Restaurant; Laura Carter of Mrs. Carter's; Executive Chef Louise Duhamel and Manager Martin Stitt of Langdon Hall; Chef Tim Erskine and General Manager Gary Burroughs of the Oban Inn; Executive Chef Patissier Ernst Frehner, Sandi Digras and Deneen Perrin of the Château Laurier; Gail Groen and Judy Luft of The Emporium; Jackie Enticknapp and Holly Woelfle of Petticoat Parlour; Executive Chef George McNeill, Kerry Shepherd and Meryl Baron of the Royal York Hotel; Executive Chef Timothy K. Mullin and Manager Patrick Boutette of the Doctor's House; Marlene Percy of the Morriston Tea Room; Anne Riddall of McGregor House; and Pat Young of Eagleview Manor. I am also grateful to Catharine Gray for permission to quote from the diary of Frances Gay Simpson, and to Lenore Law for permission to use the photograph of Rosina Eliza Crossweller and Louisa Cowell.

For their assistance and encouragement with research aspects of this project, I thank Barbara Aitken of the Stauffer Library, Queen's University; Susan Bellingham of the University of Waterloo Archives; Maureen Dolyniuk of the Hudson's Bay Company Archives; Leon Warmski and Christine Bourolias of the Archives of Ontario; Teresa Milne Tait of Kingston; Fiona Lucas of the Toronto Historical Board and Richard Feltoe, Toronto. I am also grateful to Eaton's for permission to use materials from the Eaton Collection. I also thank Ryan Taylor, of the Allen County Public Library, for his endless enthusiasm and years of fabulous tea times; Judith and Nellie Noble for always making it fun; Mary and Ted Gallagher, tea brewers par excellence; my daughter, Sarah, for assisting in the kitchen; and to my husband, Peter, for his infinite support.

ACKNOWLEDGMENTS

I am grateful to Barry Penhale, my publisher, for his encouragement and support and to Jane Gibson for editing tips. And for years of faithful tea-drinking companionship I thank the many friends who have always made time for tea. To my family, my relatives and those ancestors who set me on the pathway to tea-time pleasures, I owe everything.

Contents

Note to the Reader

It is impossible for me to overstate the value I place upon the institution of afternoon tea. From the instant I was permitted, as a young child, to join my mother and grandmother in the pleasures of tea time, I was captivated by the tremendous feeling of emotional well-being so naturally induced by the process of relaxing and chatting over a pot of tea.

Since leaving England thirty years ago to take up residence in Canada, my family tea time tradition has remained strong. It was while entertaining Old Order Mennonite neighbours to afternoon tea and being exposed to the influences of their simpler and quieter lives, that I was inspired to begin learning about the ways in which women of the past had spent their leisure time, particularly with reference to afternoon tea.

Exploring commercial tea rooms has provided an additional dimension to this pleasurable pastime. In a special way I have come to know many of Ontario's towns by combining visits to local tea rooms with learning more about those communities. There is, of course, still room for more tea rooms. I particularly look forward to the day when I can plan to take afternoon tea at Kingston. Local folks still talk of the splendid tea room which closed its doors many years ago.

Being steeped in this tradition since childhood, I naturally have very high standards when it comes to the tea table. So I have featured my favourite places to take tea in Ontario. I should stress that I include only those establishments which totally fulfill my expectations. I would also like to point out how enormously grateful I am to the chefs and proprietors of these establishments for generously sharing their special recipes, thereby allowing readers of this publication to prepare their own sumptuous afternoon teas. My hope is that this book will provide a glimpse into the delights of tea times, past and present, and go some way towards ensuring the continuation of this marvellous tradition.

STEEPED IN TRADITION

Tea with Granny

Come, little cottage girl, you seem
To want my cup of tea;
and will you take a little cream?
Now tell the truth to me.

BARRY PAIN

I began drinking tea early in life and now look upon my enjoyment of tea time as a treasured legacy from my grandmother. Granny's motto was: "Nothing welcomes like a fresh pot of tea set on a beautifully arranged table." Her words still ring through my mind no matter whether I happen to be taking tea in the Lakelands of England, the west coast of Canada or in one of the many splendid tea rooms of Ontario.

We lived in Lancashire, where, as in the rest of Britain, tea time is an institution. At three o'clock sharp every weekday afternoon, Granny would busy herself in her scullery and brew a pot of tea. Then, carrying her teapot in one hand and her special teacup and saucer in the other, she carefully negotiated the red brick path which led from her door to ours. Her arrival signaled the beginning of a special time. She and Mother would settle down together. For the next hour the outside world would cease to be.

Afternoon tea during the week was always shared with Granny. It was a ritual I thoroughly enjoyed. My reward for good behaviour was to be given my very own teacup. It was a half-size cup and, at an age far too young to remember, I mastered drinking from it. A thin stream of weak tea, drowned in sufficient milk to disguise any flavour, together with a sandwich, a biscuit or perhaps a sliver of cake, had the amazing effect of reinforcing good behaviour and making me feel very grown up. However, what made this important was not just the fun of learning how to doctor my tea without spilling the milk and the excitement of exploring savoury or sweet delights. It was most precious because there was no rush. We all had time for each other. The conversation of little people was just as important as that of the adults, and the resulting flow of ideas and concerns did more than anything else to bond all of us together. No matter what else might be interrupted or postponed during the course of the day, we knew that we could always count on tea time. It was sacrosanct.

The tradition of sharing tea with Granny was borne, I suspect, out of a need for economy during war-time Britain. When so many things were rationed, frugality dictated that a pot of tea must be shared. I remember that when I was still quite young, I would hurry home from school, hoping to find Granny still seated at the tea table so that I would not miss taking part in what had become an important family custom. The tea experience became so much a part of my life that, like the young daughter of Charles Darwin who questioned her companions about where *their* fathers did *their* barnacles, I would ask, "And what time does *your* Granny come to tea?" It took me a while to realize that not all children had grandmothers who came to tea.

My father's afternoon tea, though far less grand than ours, was equally savoured. Each morning before leaving the house, he carefully measured out and mixed together just the right proportions of loose tea and sugar—"puttin' me brew up" was his description of this task. He took this mixture with him when he left for work, carefully twisted into several thicknesses of newspaper. Dad used an old medicine bottle, complete with a cork stopper, to hold milk. It also served as his milk jug. To avoid carrying milk, some people added a dollop of condensed milk to their tea and sugar mixture. This created a really sticky mess which necessitated lots of scraping of the newspaper when it came time to brew the tea. One cannot help but wonder just how much printers' ink was consumed by British workman using this method. Printers' ink or not, three o'clock tea time provided a refreshing pause, not just for my father, but for workmen all across the nation. It was a time of renewing the spirits before the last chores of the day were commenced and it offered a brief period for chit-chat. It was not only blue-collar workers who paused for tea. Bankers, clergy and office workers did too. In fact, all over the land, the British public settled down to take tea. By sharing this time with family, friends or colleagues, the continuance of this famous British institution was ensured.

My parents had a favourite blend of tea, marketed under the name Black and Green's. This tea, though one of the economy blends, had a remarkably good flavour. Besides its good taste, there was additional incentive for the housewives of post-war Britain to purchase it. Labels could be clipped from the quarter pound packages, collected and redeemed from the producer for all sorts of useful household items. Mother was kept in tea towels for years by drinking Black and Green's.

Our teapot had a place of honour in the kitchen. It was a large Brown Betty, and although used up to ten times a day, it was always treated with a great deal of respect. Mother had strict rules; the inside of the pot was never to be washed in soapy water. After use, it was simply rinsed under running water. Consequently, a buildup of brown tannin stained the inside of the pot. In many Lancashire homes, this was considered to be as essential to a good teapot as was a spout that poured well. Therefore, breaking a teapot was truly a calamity, for it would take weeks to "season" a new pot. But gradually a brown lining would appear. In time, the new pot would become as highly prized as its predecessor and could be counted upon to produce the perfect "cuppa."

It was the custom to lace cups of tea with tots of whiskey in some abodes in Lancashire. This was not a practice to which my family adhered. Perhaps because of their views, I agreed that it was a totally ridiculous, not to say expensive, way of ruining a good cup of tea. However, at festive times of the year, such as Christmas, most homes kept the whiskey, or in some instances the rum bottle, close to the teapot. One smiled, at times, to hear elderly matrons expounding upon the habits of "good old Queen Vickie, God bless her soul", who, it was said, also enjoyed the odd tipple in the teacup.

Granny and her sisters were children of the Victorian era. All which that age entailed, in terms of traditions and etiquette, was dear to them. These women held a certain fascination for me. For there was much that was "old fashioned" about them. Even their language, at times, was different from my own. They often used words, now long forgotten, except by those who strive to preserve Lancashire dialect and terminology. Granny's kitchen, for example, was always her "scullery", and her sink, the "slopstone."

Granny's sister Hannah had "gone into service" as they called it in England—meaning she cooked, kept house, and did whatever other household duties were required of her by her employer. She became an excellent cook and eventually she married a farmer. During my mother's youth, Aunt Hannah and Uncle Henry farmed at Lathkill House, Alport, in the peak district of Derbyshire, a property belonging to the Duke of Rutland. While living there, Aunt Hannah earned extra income by providing visitors to the district with afternoon tea. Few would arrive by car. Most were ramblers and walkers, who after a full day of hiking in the Pennines, brought healthy appetites to the tea table—filling up on scones, fruitcake and other delectable treats, all washed down by gallons of tea. Some of these traditional teatime recipes from Aunt Hannah as well as those of my grandmother are included in the recipe section.

For as long as I can remember, afternoon tea has been my favourite meal. Indeed, I have always loved every aspect of the teatime tradition, whether supping by the fireside on cold winter days or taking part in outdoor summer tea parties. However, it is not just the food and drink that makes this institution so pleasurable. It goes much deeper than this. For generations teatime has provided a vehicle in which people could become better acquainted. How many secrets have been shared and how many hearts have been eased, while chatting with a sympathetic companion over a cup of tea? Those who are already devotees of the afternoon tea tradition will agree that it has been more than tea and delicious food which ensured the continuance of this time-honoured institution. The calming effect of settling down with a warm steamy beverage has long been appreciated. When we add companionship and relaxation to this, we have the basic ingredients for creating and enhancing the bonds of friendship. It is not surprising that the ritual of tea taking is well established in a host of different cultures.

On a warm spring day, shortly before my grandson's second birthday, I set the tea tray and carried it outdoors. We settled ourselves on the deck. Cups and saucers were handed round. Tea was poured. Joel, seated in his little chair, rested his chin on his hand and said, "Now, Grandma, what shall we talk about?" In that instant, I knew that Joel, as young as he was, had already absorbed the essence of tea time. Yes, the tradition will continue.

In the Beginning

~~~~

*"There is a great deal of poetry and
fine sentiment in a chest of tea."*
RALPH WALDO EMERSON

Tea has a very interesting history. It is thought that the
first writing on this subject by a European was that of
the Venetian, Giovanni Botero, who wrote a book called *On
The Causes of Greatness in Cities*. This treatise, published in
1589, contained a good deal of information about tea drinking. Naturally, it whetted the Italian appetite for this new and
exotic beverage. It was, however, another decade before the
British public was presented with its opportunity for enlight-
enment. Curiosity was piqued by the English translation of
Jan Hugo van Linschooten's book on travels in the Orient.
Through this volume, arm-chair travellers were privy to the
adventurous escapades of Dutch sailors who, amongst other
things, related tales of tea drinking in China and Japan.[1]

Over the years, many curious tales have been recited regarding the early history of tea in Britain. One Victorian
legend suggested that two pounds of tea were presented as a
gift to royalty. It was then looked upon as a new and curious
vegetable and came in the form of crisp, dried, rolled up
leaves, which were carefully boiled and served at the royal
table with salt, pepper and melted butter. The liquid in
which it was boiled was thrown away. Not surprisingly, the
leaves were pronounced "too tough to eat." Others attribute
the arrival of tea to a British admiral who discovered it in
the galley of a Dutch vessel which he had captured.

Research suggests it is the Dutch who had introduced tea to
Holland and France after having discovered it during trading

missions to China. French nobility had then rather taken to it. In fact, it became popular amongst many wealthy Europeans years before the British were even aware of tea.

By the mid 1600's small amounts of tea began trickling into England from Europe largely through the famed East India Trading Company. But it was not in general use until the end of the century. To begin with, it was rather scarce and also very expensive. In fact, the price of tea in 1657 was greater than that of 1980. Obviously people such as my ancestors, who were very ordinary folk, would have waited a long time before being able to afford to taste this new beverage.

Governments of all ages share one thing in common— they never let a good thing pass. And so it was with the British government of the day. Once they caught on to the fact that people were clamoring to purchase tea, they implemented taxes upon its import and even resorted to taxing the infusion of it in water by the gallon, in common with chocolate and sherbet. As you can imagine, this encouraged all sorts of exciting events up and down the coastline. Ships from Holland would rest off-shore awaiting the arrival of British smugglers, who, in the dead of night, rowed out to retrieve their illicit wares. Liquor, tobacco and tea and whatever other items could be acquired were stashed away in caves until being sold or passed on to others.

Upon occasion these escapades turned nasty. Still a significant number of people held to the opinion that outwitting the excise men was rather fun. Smugglers and excise men led each other on a merry chase. Every coastal community had its heroes. Tales of triumph became legends to be savoured over booze at the local inns. Contraband tea filtered its way into all manner of homes, often serving as bribes or as thanks for favours received. Many a clergyman, though perhaps unwittingly, enjoyed his morning tea due to the efforts of his local smugglers.

When Catherine of Braganza, daughter of John IV of Portugal, married Charles II, she set about introducing tea to

English court life. It is said that her first request, upon landing in England in 1662, was for a cup of tea. Since tea was already quite popular in Portugal, Catherine had grown accustomed to this new beverage. Later she would derive what comfort she could from its flavour and warmth. Long evenings of loneliness were averted as the ladies of the court chatted over tea cups while Catherine's husband, amorous creature that he was, was generally off cavorting with Nell Gwynn, Lucy Walter or other of his various mistresses.

Outside of court life, tea was only available in the coffee houses of London. General consensus was that women were not to frequent these places. And so it was necessary for them to sample tea in the privacy of the home. Samuel Pepys wrote in his diary in June 1667: "By coach home and there to find my wife making of tea, a drink which Mr. Pelling the pothecary tells her is good for her cold and defluxions."[2] Obviously, this new and exotic commodity was thought, at least by some, to contain medicinal qualities. In some quarters, tea was advertised as having properties which would cure headaches, giddiness, and in fact, almost any complaint or ill.

Before one hundred years had passed, the supping of tea had become so popular that elegant and genteel tea houses began opening their doors to both sexes. In the words of Frederick Dane and R. S. McIndoe, "Sketches of high life in the reign of Queen Ann [1702-1714] show us the high-born dames of that period congregating in the fashionable teahouses and sipping the beverage from Oriental china cups."[3]

Fashionable youngsters were also caught up in this new pastime. The ability to entertain school chums with tea assumed paramount importance amongst wealthy schoolboys. In 1766, William Dutton wrote home from Eton college to his father in Sherborne, "I wish you would be so kind as to let me have tea and sugar to drink in the afternoon, without which there is no keeping company with other boys of my standing."[4] Whether the boys snacked on plum cake as they relished their tea is not known. But, if present-day habits are anything to go by, the cookie tin was probably not too far away.

Although poets and others soon began to sing the praises of tea, not everybody agreed with them. Some spoke against it. Some went as far as to claim that tea drinking was impoverishing the nation. They compared it to a slow poison and also suggested that it was bad for morals. But Samuel Johnson took issue. He proclaimed in a magazine of the day that he was, "A hardened and shameless tea-drinker who has for many years diluted his meals with only the infusion of this fascinating plant; whose kettle has scarcely time to cool; who with tea amuses the evening, with tea solaces the midnight, and with tea welcomes the morning."[5] Who could argue with praise such as this? Very few apparently since before the 18th century was done, tea had become the national beverage of Britain.

It was around 1840, legend tells, that Anna, the 7th Duchess of Bedford, when feeling rather peckish one afternoon, ordered sandwiches and cake along with her regular afternoon cup of tea. It became a habit. Some would have considered the Duchess' new-found pleasure to be nothing more than a greedy self–indulgence. But they were soon swallowing their objections, along with their own cake and tea. Thanks to Anna, afternoon tea had arrived!

There was, of course, a perfectly valid reason for the Duchess to desire a late afternoon pick-me-up. The truth was that she was just about starving by that time. In those days the custom was to eat a relatively small breakfast, very little lunch and a huge dinner late in the evening. It is no wonder that the poor woman was flagging by four o'clock. Consider the fact that little, if any, was understood about balancing food groups in order to achieve a healthy diet. Given this lack of knowledge, most people went around suffering from a whole array of disorders caused by mild to chronic dietary insufficiencies. By mid-afternoon most of the population was probably beginning to feel a little droopy.

Whether the coming of the afternoon tea habit had any bearing upon remedying problems created by poor diet is debatable. However, there is no doubt that by raising the blood sugar levels of these wilting violets, and thereby providing them with sufficient energy to get them through the rest of the day, afternoon tea was providing a much needed service.

It took a matter of decades for afternoon tea to develop into the institution we know today in the English-speaking world. It began with the aristocracy. But in due course, it filtered down to became a part of the lives of ordinary people. Perhaps it was celebrated with less pomp and circumstance, but no doubt it was consumed with equal pleasure.

And so, as you settle down to afternoon tea, whether alone or with friends, fill up your tea cups and drink a toast to Anna, Duchess of Bedford. Rest assured that her whim was not just a greedy indulgence. May this wonderful institution last through many more generations.

Visits and Tea

"Strong tea and scandal—Bless me how refreshing."
RICHARD BRINSLEY SHERIDAN

Once people became accustomed to drinking tea on a regular basis, they were inclined to become quite grumpy when they had to do without. In fact, there were many who simply could not cope without their daily ration of tea. Tea was carted off to battle during military campaigns. The Duke of Wellington is said to have drunk tea as readily on the battlefield as he did in the fashionable drawing rooms of London. Royalty drank it. Politicians loved it. William Gladstone is reputed to have filled his hot-water bottle with the stuff—just in case he needed an emergency supply during the night. Possibly this story is stretching the truth a little, but Gladstone did profess to drink more tea between the hours of midnight and four a.m. than any other member of the British Commons. Tea also travelled with explorers, off to chart distant lands. And, of course, it came to Canada, carefully shipped by the Hudson's Bay Company.

According to Hudson's Bay Company records, the first shipment of tea to Canada was made on June 7, 1715, when "3 cannisters of Bohea tea" were shipped aboard the frigate *Hudson's Bay* , under the command of Captain Joseph Davis.[6] They were consigned to Governor James Knight at York Factory. However, because of bad weather, the ship was forced to put back to England without reaching the bay. Captain Davis' higher ups were not pleased. In fact, they thought so little of his efforts that they promptly dismissed him from the service. Not until the next year did the same three cannisters of tea finally reach North America. They travelled on the same ship, but obviously under the command of a different captain. In view of what was in store for Governor Knight, we can only hope that he brewed his Bohea to perfection and that he relished it to the very last drop.

Three years later, the same James Knight became the officer in command when crews of the *Albany* and of the *Discovery* set sail together on their ill fated "Northern Discovery Expedition."[7] They took with them six pounds of tea, valued at £6, which the frigate *Albany* had brought from England especially for use on the expedition. The object of this voyage was to search for minerals, and if possible, to find traces of the long sought after north-west passage, the "Straights of Anian." Neither vessel returned. Almost fifty years would pass before another Hudson's Bay Company vessel, out on a whaling trip, discovered bones and other artifacts, proving that the two ships had been trapped by ice near Marble Island.

The old adage, "beggars can't be choosers", was certainly apt in those days of precarious shipping. People simply had to make do with what came their way. It seems that Bohea tea, though eagerly awaited by Governor Knight, was far from the best tea in the world. The Canadian Department of Agriculture later described it as "...the poorest kind of black tea, mixed with dust and large flat brown and brownish-green leaves. The liquor was a dark brownish-red, and always left a black sediment in the cup."[8]

While early immigrants to Canada looked forward to the arrival of all provisions, the arrival of tea, poor quality or not, was particularly important. Even in the midst of war and out on campaign, there were some decencies of life that were to be maintained if one were to call oneself civilized. T.G. Ridout, an officer in the War of 1812, serving in the Militia forces on the Niagara frontier wrote on September 4, 1813;

"We collect balm from the garden for tea [because real tea was virtually unattainable except at a King's ransom]...extensive robbery of peas, onion, corn, carrots etc., for we can get nothing but by stealing except milk. Bread and butter is out of the question. We have an iron pot which serves for teapot, roaster, and boiler and two window shutters...for a table..."[9]

In pioneering days, when distances were so vast and travelling so difficult, visits from friends or from strangers were especially important. Many people lived in relative isolation and would seize whatever opportunities they could to socialize with others. Under these circumstances, tea came to represent a warmth and hospitality reminiscent of life in the old country. Explorer Charles Francis Hall, while at Northumberland Inlet during the mid 1860's, was pleasantly surprised when his hostess offered him a cup of tea. "Before I was aware of it, Tookoolito had the 'tea-kettle' over the friendly fire-lamp, and the water boiling. She asked me if I drank tea. Imagine my surprise at this, the question coming from an Esquimaus in an Esquimaux tent! I replied, 'I do; but you have not tea here, have you?' Drawing her hand from a little tin box, she displayed it full of fine-flavored black tea, saying, 'Do you like your tea strong?' Thinking to spare her the use of much of this precious article away up here, far from the land of civilization, I replied, 'I'll take it weak, if you please.' A cup of hot tea was soon before me — capital tea, and capitally made. Taking from my pocket a sea-biscuit which I had brought from the vessel for my dinner, I shared it with my hostess. Seeing she had but one cup, I induced her to share with me its contents. There, amid the snows of the North, under an Esquimaux's hospitable tent, in the company with Esquimaux, for the first time I shared with them in that soothing, cheering, invigorating emblem of civilization — T-E-A."[10]

Tea, therefore, took on the same importance for the new settlers as it had for their parents and grandparents in Britain and Europe. Nothing warmed the cockles of the hearts of immigrants better than a steaming cup of tea. Sharing a pot with a few friends, or with a roomful, provided a setting for exchanging confidences, for gossiping and for mulling over the difficulties and joys of life.

The tea-pot became a constant companion, offering solace, pleasure and comfort. In the late 1790's, Mrs. Simcoe often wrote in her journal of taking tea. No matter whether she was in Québec, Montreal, York (Toronto) or Niagara, Elizabeth Simcoe always had several tea-drinking companions.[11] Other diarists also wrote of tea. In September of 1837, while residing near Fenelon Falls, Anne Langton reflected upon the difficulty of obtaining supplies such as tea and rice, suggesting that these provisions might more easily be found on Lake Ontario rather than on the store shelves.[12] This was a problem well understood by merchants of the day. They sympathized with the frustrations of their customers and did their best to ensure that they kept their shelves well stocked. But they, too, were at the mercy of suppliers, and of the elements. Winter blizzards, ocean storms and poor inland transportation systems all conspired against healthy stocks of tea.

Gradually the number of shipments of tea and tea accoutrements increased. Before long, obtaining tea rations became something most people would take for granted. Anne Langton may have had some difficulty obtaining provisions at Fenelon Falls, but Canniff Haight was of the opinion that by the 1820's, Canadians, so far as eating and drinking were concerned, fared ... "sumptuously every day." ... "Their breakfast not unfrequently consists of twelve or fourteen different ingredients, which are of the most heterogeneous nature. Green tea and fried pork, honey comb and salted salmon, pound cake and pickled cucumbers, stewed chickens and apple-tarts, maple molasses and pease-pudding, gingerbread and sourcrout, are to be found at almost every table. The dinner differs not at all from the breakfast, and the afternoon repast, which they term supper, is equally substantial."[13]

Green tea was much in use at this time. Later in the century, it would come under criticism, even amongst some medics, as being injurious to the nerves and stomach. This, along with concerns about the possibility of green tea being adulterated by the addition of imitation teas or fragments of rice and paddy-husks, conspired to lower its consumption.

The more affluent of Canada's early settlers would have brought fancy tea services and china along with them when they arrived. They used them with pride. However, prior to the mid-1800's, most people lived a pioneering style of life and did not have such luxuries. When they could afford to purchase tea, they were not able to brew and serve it in an elegant drawing room fashion. For them, an old iron pot would heat the water, then a sprinkle of tea leaves would be added. The pot might be topped up with water, over and over again. Additional leaves would be flung in when necessary. The resulting beverage soon became strong enough to trot a mouse on and would certainly deteriorate in flavour as the day wore on. The taste may have left much to be desired, but once it was served up it was still good for warming up a body and for dunking crullers. It also worked wonders for softening up bread crusts for the toothless.

While it was predominantly Dutch and English colonists who introduced tea to the New World, an enterprising young Scotsman named Thomas J. Lipton was largely responsible for popularizing the beverage in North America. Already he had established a successful tea business throughout England, based on a commitment to sell only the freshest, highest quality blend of leaves to produce the unique tea taste he pioneered. Lipton brought those leaves and his potential tea blend to America on his personal fleet of clipper ships from his own tea estates in Ceylon (now Sri Lanka).

By bringing tea from garden to grocer, Lipton was able to supply his blend at a more reasonable price and thereby increase the demand for Lipton tea. He was also the first to package tea in small convenient tins to keep it fresh and preserve the flavour. This also would ensure that customers received an accurate measure of tea leaves. Largely through his entrepeneurial skills, Lipton ensured that tea would become the most popular drink on both sides of the Atlantic.[14]

On February 14, 1885, William "Tiger" Dunlop drew up his Last Will and Testament. The will was so full of irreverent remarks that some of his associates thought he had gone too far. "I leave John Caddle a silver teapot, to the end that he may drink tea therefrom to comfort him under the affliction of a slatternly wife."[15]

It is hoped that the acquisition of a silver teapot compensated Mrs. Caddle for being on the receiving end of such unkind words.

We know, from reading the diaries and journals of our forefathers, that a significant number of people were already settled into a relatively comfortable lifestyle by the mid-1840's. Among this group would be the clergy. Anglican clergymen in particular, along with their families, were being sent out from Britain to minister to the immigrants. With this small group came middle class values and middle class habits. Of course, tea time was part of their world.

From Susanna Moodie, one of the most prolific recorders of the pioneer days comes this tribute to tea: "Goat Island, The cup of excellent tea was most refreshing after the fatigues of the day; and, while enjoying it, I got into an agreeable const with several pleasant people, but we were all strangers even in name to each other."[16]

The following instructions for setting the tea table are attributed to Catherine (Geddes) Macaulay, the wife of Rev. William Macaulay of Picton, Ontario. They were written two years prior to her death in 1849.

The High Tea Table

Let a pure white cloth be neatly laid; let the tray be covered with a white napkin; and on it, as for breakfast, the sugar, cream, and slop-basin, containing the spoons and the cups and saucers within them. Let it be placed in the middle of one side or at the end. Put around the tables as many small plates as may be wanted, with a small knife in front of each, or at its side; at the end or side, opposite the tray, let the dish of ripe or stewed fruit be set, with a large spoon and a pile of small saucers in front or at the side of it. On the other side, some little distance from it, let there be plates, with bread sliced, about the eighth of an inch in thickness; or let one dish be of hot wigs, or rusk, or tea-biscuit. Let a fine mold of butter occupy the centre of the table; let its knife be beside it; and on each side a small plate, the one with cold meat, ham, or tongue, sliced thin. The other with sliced cheese, or a fresh pot-cheese. A pitcher of ice-water, with small tumblers surrounding it, may occupy one corner, and a basket or plate of cake the other. Or a glass-dish of custard may occupy the place mentioned for the fruit, and the fruit may be distributed in small saucers, with fine white sugar heaped on the centre of each and placed upon each plate: this gives the table a very pretty appearance. Or, the custard baked in small cups, may occupy the places for the saucers of fruit. The same appurtenances, with the addition of forke, are requisite, with perhaps an urn of coffee, for winter tea-table.[17]

When we think about what we loosely term "the Victorian period," or of things generally associated with this era, we find that it is mostly the latter period of Queen Victoria's reign which comes to mind. Victoria was crowned on June 28, 1838. It was a time when most Canadians had to work very hard in order to keep body and soul together. At this time in our history, most people did not have economic resources sufficient to acquire the finer things in life. Those beautiful old Victorian homes, which are so admired today, were not much in evidence in the 1840's and 50's. But the age of industry was gaining fast. By the 1860's and 70's money was being made.

The success of their tannery business, founded in 1857, provided a lifestyle of comfort for the Breithaupt family of Berlin [now Kitchener]. Their story is one of prominence gained through business and political achievements. It is a story repeated over and over as towns began to thrive. While business ventures and the daily concerns of family life differed from family to family, the Breithaupts had much in common with leading families all over the province. The Breithaupts were also wonderful diarists and documented their activities beautifully.

On November 21, 1867, twelve year old Louis J. Breithaupt, who would later become President of the Breithaupt Leather Company, wrote in his diary: "Grandmother promised me 2 shillings if I would get up at 4 o'clock, start the fire and put the tea kettle on."[18]

Obviously Louis' mother did not think too highly of this notion, for the following day's entry reads: "I didn't succeed. Mother said, if I were to start the fire and put on the tea kettle then the hired girl could give me 2 shillings a week."[19]

The "tea" theme is constant throughout Breithaupt family diaries and is frequently central to family celebrations. Seventeen years later, on August 16, 1884, the family gathered for a happy event. Louis wrote: "To-day was Ma's 50th birth-day. She & the rest of the Penetang party arrived home early this week. Aunt Raquet from Detroit with two of her children also arrived here about a week ago. Ma's birthday was celebrated by a 'tea' on the lawn this evening. The good wishes & presents were numerous. Ma's health at present is better than it has been for years."[20]

The Victorian era provided just the right setting for afternoon tea. Over-stuffed furniture, crammed into overly decorated rooms, created nooks and crannies naturally conducive to gossipy tête-à-têtes. Add to this the Victorians' fascination with gadgets and knick-knacks—many of which were devised for the ceremony of tea—and we have the perfect setting for those famous Victorian drawing-room tea parties.

By the 1860's, the tradition of entertaining with tea, in the fullest sense, was becoming firmly established in Ontario. For the affluent, visiting and the receiving of visitors was very much connected with the serving of tea. Drawing rooms of the wealthy often mirrored those of Britain and Europe. Filling their homes with all sorts of accoutrements, Victorian housekeepers set great store in presenting just the right image. Attention was paid to the finest detail.

Eventually a whole business of etiquette grew around the institution of tea. For instance, from the mid-Victorian period onwards, especially for people in society, there was rather an important component of social etiquette woven into the institution of afternoon tea. "It was simply not considered proper to give a tea if one owed any social calls. Therefore, a good

Lady Agnes Macdonald's drawing room at Earnscliffe, Ottawa, set for a cozy tea. *National Archives of Canada*

hostess would be sure that she had done all the visiting required of her before she organised her tea. Once the tea had taken place, she would then owe a visit to everyone who had attended. To simplify the matter of trying to remember who had attended her tea, all of the guests would have left their calling cards. This way, one was able to check exactly who had attended and to whom one owed a call."[21]

There was also the question of what to wear at a tea party. If a woman was from a well-to-do background, she would pay close attention to such fashion dictates. During the late Victorian period, an ordinary woman might own an "afternoon tea frock" which would be a fairly simple elegant dress suitable for wear during day visits. Society women, on the other hand, had the choice of wearing a carriage dress, (but only if they were arriving at their destination by horse and carriage), or a morning dress, walking dress or visiting dress, (if arriving on foot). Obviously women from less affluent backgrounds were not in a position to concern themselves with such things. M. Loane quotes a Victorian woman as saying, "I envy the poor, it must be so delightful not to have to think about appearances."[22] This statement possibly sums up the degree of frustration wealthy women found when it came to having to make decisions about which outfit to wear for which occasion. It also indicates how out-of-touch these folk were, when it came to really understanding about the lives of the poor.

When a tea had been planned, it was a matter of making sure that appropriate staff were on hand to assist. Those who were lucky enough to have competent and cooperative servants were very fortunate indeed. Many were not. However, even with good staff, complications could arise. Imagine the annoyance of a young servant whose afternoon off was cancelled simply because the mistress decided to entertain with tea. In such instances it was only natural to expect some degree of pouting. But, if the mistress were kindly, she would make it up to the servant at a later date. Or in some cases, the annoyance could arise from the "borrowing" of staff, as recorded by Mary Elizabeth Lucy Ronalds Harris on May 7, 1869. "Called on Rebecca, Rhea and Miss Beddina. I could not ask them to tea as Mrs. Harris wanted both my servants for a dinner party. I should have thought one would have [been] enough at a time. I was very sorry it so happened."[23]

When servants got into the "Mountain Dew", instead of the tea pot, serious complications arose. Drunkenness was not uncommon. Naturally it threatened the long term relationship between a mistress and her servant. Needless to say, such mischief created havoc in the kitchen, as well as amongst the guests.

Once the business of tea had become firmly entrenched into the social network of Ontario, people began planning all manner of events around drinking this delicious beverage. During the Victorian period, in addition to drawing-room tea parties, those who could afford to also gave "At Homes." These occasions, designed to accommodate many visitors, often provided a more elaborate arrangement of food than the drawing-room tea. The lady of the house usually enlisted her daughters to pour tea, coffee or cocoa. If there were no daughters, other young women were pressed into doing this. Still others would be needed to pass things round. Generally speaking, the prettier these young women were, the better. Etiquette books of the day suggested that a "charming" married woman may pour, if there were no young ladies available.

For a true attempt at formality, an array of tasks would be assigned. The door must be answered and cloaks removed. Somebody was responsible for replenishing sandwiches, cakes and the tea-pots. A clean-up crew was also essential for clearing away used items. "At Homes" were extremely popular because they provided the hostess with the opportunity of paying back a large number of social obligations all at once.

This was the era of the "calling card," a system cleverly devised to simplify the business of inviting guests for teas and other social occasions. One merely sent, or delivered, one's calling card with the message "Tea at 4 o'clock" or "At Home 6 p.m."

Mrs. Peter J. Milne
Friday, January 18th

Tea at 4 o'clock

Guests were expected to be punctual. One arrived no sooner than five minutes before the hour and no later than five minutes after the hour. *The Home Cook Book*, published in Toronto in 1877, suggests that "the tea is brought in punctually and placed on the hostess' table in the corner, where are the urns of black, green and Russian tea for those who like each, a basket of wafers, delicate sandwiches of chicken or thin sliced meats, and a basket of fancy cake. If the English style is followed, the cups of tea are carried to the guests on a tray, and a tiny table to rest the cups on placed in reach of each group."[24] Harlequin tea service, meaning cups of various designs, were popular for this kind of a tea.

Those in society received an endless sequence of invitations. For these people, it became necessary to devote one or two days per week solely to visiting. It was not uncommon for society women to pay up to fifteen calls in one day. Tea might be offered at each call and, since guests could not politely refuse what was offered, one can only wonder at the level of caffeine coursing through the veins of these social creatures, let alone the state of their bladders.

Naturally, the formality commanded by grand occasions was not reflected in smaller, less wealthy homes. Similarly, those living in rural areas would also have a less rigid approach to entertaining with tea. If the lady of the house did not have a particular day when she "received," one might pay her a visit at any time and expect to be given a cup of tea.

Very few Canadians had the pleasure of enjoying private tea parties with Queen Victoria. However, once a year, when she and the Queen were both in Scotland, the Canadian prima donna, Emma Albani, was honoured in this way. The following account was written in the *Manitoba Morning Free Press.*

"The tea drinking occasion is wholly devoid of pomp and circumstance. The Queen drinks her beverage which, by the way, is English breakfast, quite like an ordinary mortal, but, quite unlike the ordinary English woman, she does not take a second cup. The honour of serving tea to her majesty is one seldom accorded to other subjects. For Albani, the Queen had always had a particular affection, and she delights to honour her in various ways. Upon these occasions of the afternoon function the Queen sends word a day or two previously of her intention to visit her neighbour. She is accompanied by one of the princesses, and a lady or two in waiting, and she drives the distance of about ten miles in an open carriage. After the brief ceremony of tea drinking is over, the Queen takes a stroll through her hostess' beautiful garden. Although not particularly fond of flowers, she appreciates Mme. Albani's fondness for them and frequently sends her superb bouquets from Balmoral. The Queen's dress is usually very simple—a black cashmere or soft silk."[25]

There is no doubt that taking tea is far more pleasurable for today's women than it was for their Victorian counterparts. How, we might ask, could we possibly enjoy an afternoon tea if it were necessary to appear at the tea table encased in a pair of tightly laced stays, or be forced to sit on the edge of a seat in order to protect our bustles? Besides the physical discomforts of wearing garments which, though designed to flatter the figure, were often injurious to health, the poor women of long ago also had to learn how to acquire the art of seeming not to enjoy their food. Sighs of ecstasy, which we often hear as teeth bite into succulent sandwiches and delicious cakes, would never have squeezed past the lips of those high society Victorian lasses who were so well schooled in manners. They were expected to nibble daintily on tiny morsels, all the while pretending to have no interest in the food itself. Eating was, in the opinion of some, just another of those vulgar bodily functions. Fortunately, such silliness has long passed.

Tea was often purchased in quite large quantities. In January of 1881, Frances Gay Simpson, of Hamilton, recorded in her diary, "ten pounds of tea brought in."[26] Mrs. Simpson very likely purchased this tea locally, but within a few years, T. Eaton and Co., was offering an excellent selection of teas, "put up in lead packages and guaranteed absolutely pure," through their 1890-91 catalogue.[27] The teas were marketed in assorted grades, good, better and best. Eaton's also advertised Basket Fried Japan tea, "which leaves were roasted in a wire basket over a fire", Hyson tea, and China Congou tea — "the tea that contains the least tannin of any black tea."[28] They also sold Gunpowder tea, suggesting two ounces be added to any of their ordinary black tea blends. Similarly, one ounce of Formosa Oolong was reputed to enhance flavour when added to any black blend.

Everybody had a preference when it came to tea or blends of teas. Those who could afford to would have kept several teas on hand, favouring them for various times of the day. Some hostesses became quite famous for their blends of tea.

But planning a tea party involved a little more than merely selecting which tea to serve. Edibles also had to be decided upon. The Victorians had a surprisingly sweet tooth. It takes no more than a glance at cookbooks of the day to confirm this. They were interested in all manner of sweets. Cakes of all sorts were very popular. The Victoria sandwich cake, named in honour of Queen Victoria, is our legacy from this era. Scones were also very important items and were often served at breakfast as well as tea time. For the tea table, fancy sandwiches were concocted from a wide variety of things. One of the more unusual sandwich fillings of this age was shredded nasturtium flowers. With the addition of a few tender seeds, they were thought to be very special. Another interesting sandwich filling was concocted from finely chopped preserved ginger and candied orange peel, mixed with thick cream. Sandwiches could be filled with almost anything, from fruits, such as dates, to baked beans or even Devonshire cream.

The New Galt Cookbook published in 1898 suggested that bread for afternoon tea sandwiches "may be fresh baked and so thinly cut with a sharp knife that the sandwiches can be rolled and each one tied with a ribbon. All crusts removed."[29] No doubt, these tiny ribbon tied sandwiches would look very pretty, but they do sound like a lot of work. Perhaps the effort was worthwhile, since they were considered to make a "pretty variety in serving sandwiches at an afternoon tea."[30]

Advertisement taken from *A Sketch of the Growth and History of Tea and the Science of Blending Particularly Adapted to the Canadian Trade. University of Waterloo Archives*

The food served at an afternoon tea was always important, but so too was the setting. If possible, teas to which large numbers of guests were expected would be served in a room other than the drawing-room, where the ladies might be receiving guests. The dining-room was the preferred choice. *The Ladies' Home Journal*, a very popular woman's magazine, recommended that two low tables, one for tea and the other for chocolate, be set. A pretty woman or charming married woman was to preside over each. "On the first of these tables, have your afternoon tea-kettle, teapot and cozy, canister, measuring-spoon, cream-jug, sugar-bowl and tongs, plates of sliced lemon and fancy cakes, cups and saucers and spoons and piles of plates and napkins. On the other let one of the chocolate-pots be placed (the purpose of its duplicate will be shown when replenishment is necessary), cups, saucers, spoons, plates, napkins, cut sugar, tongs, whipped cream and spoon, and cakes, and the arrangement of the tables for your afternoon tea will be complete."[31]

Tea not only remained within the confines of the drawing-room. Everyone drank it wherever possible. In wealthy homes, once the maids had cleared away after the family tea, it was time for the servants' tea. If the tea allowance granted by the mistress of the house was dwindling, they would simply make a brew from the still damp leaves left in the bottom of the family teapot. If they were lucky, a benevolent housekeeper might add a slice or two of bread and butter or even a sliver of cake to sustain them as they set about preparing dinner. Once the tea was over, every housemaid knew that the used tea leaves were not to be thrown away. They were saved to be used as a sweeping agent. Scattered over carpets, or even wooden floors, they helped to keep down the dust during cleaning.

An ordinary housewife or farm wife, might also find a few moments to put her feet up between chores. Perhaps a neighbour would drop in and share a spell of relaxation over a pot of tea. And then, with spirits renewed, they would part and continue getting on with the business of life.

The Victorians made much of family life, and people such as Charles Dickens contributed immensely towards creating an overwhelming degree of sentimentality. Magazines were

Advertisement taken from *A Sketch of the Growth and History of Tea and the Science of Blending Particularly Adapted to the Canadian Trade. University of Waterloo Archives*

full of elaborate drawings, articles and poems, usually depicting the activities of the "ideal" Victorian family. Generally, women were portrayed as "little homemakers" with very little to interest them apart from the running of the household. Poems such as the following one were commonplace.

Coming Home To Tea

The Fire is burning gaily
the kettle sings its best;
All things are bright and cheerful
Here in our sweet home nest,
There's nothing now, my baby,
To do for you and me,
But just to watch for some-one
coming home to tea.
We'll take our cozy places
Here in the window seat,
Where he'll be sure to spy us
Far down the chilly street,

He says it makes him warmer,
O baby just to see
the roof that we are under
When coming home to tea.[32]

Teas of one sort or another became popular from the mid 1860's until the 1960's. They were arranged for all manner of occasions. "Temperance" teas, held in even the smallest communities, provided "respectable" venues for women during the Victorian era and continued well into the 20th century. Church committees organised teas, very often as fund raising events. Rural women planned "thimble" teas where communal quilting or other projects, such as mending the children's breeches, were undertaken. And there were "kettledrum" teas, affairs comprised of much hilarity and noise, fuelled by shining urns of the amber brew and often enlivened by flirtatious young women and young men who teased them.

One of the most famous of teas was the "trousseau" tea. Food, consisting of thin bread and butter, tiny sandwiches and a few simple cakes, or a plate of cut cake was set out in a suitable room. Wedding gifts would be displayed in another. This occasion often marked the return of a bride from her honeymoon and was usually organized by the bride's mother, or some other family member. In certain circumstances, such as a bride being married far away, the trousseau tea might take place prior to the wedding. Tea was poured by the bride's mother, or by the bride's attendants. The occasion was marked by general chit-chat and the viewing of gifts. These were generally simple and elegant affairs and remained popular until the mid 20th century.

Mrs. Peter J. Milne, 10 St. Catharine Street, was hostess of a most delightfully arranged trousseau tea on Friday afternoon, Dec. 23, in honour of her daughter, Miss Carmel Milne, whose marriage takes place on Monday, Dec. 26. Mrs. Milne and her daughter received the guests in the living room, which was artisti-

Rosina Eliza Crosweller and her mother Louisa Cowell, take tea, ca. 1890. *Collection of Lenore Law*

cally adorned with quantities of chrysanthemums and roses. Mrs. Milne was wearing a handsome gown of flowered blue crepe with a corsage of pink roses and the bride-elect had chosen a lovely frock of purple velvet with a corsage of yellow roses. The artistically arranged tea table was presided over by Mrs. David McGill and Miss B. Milne and the assistants were: Mrs. W. G. Leonard, Miss G. E. Milne, Miss Kay Haley, Miss "Toots" Doyle, Miss Mildred Lawless and Miss Doris Fowler.[33]

Momentous occasions, happy or sad, usually called for a tea. Until recently, funeral teas were an important aspect of community life. Neighbours gathered at the home of the bereaved to prepare food and to brew tea for the mourners. In some cases, the funeral tea was considered to be so important that plans were carefully drawn up long before the death took place. Louis J. Breithaupt attended one such event, and wrote about it.

"Fine day. Mrs. C. Bristol, who died on Sunday was buried to-day. It was her expressed desire that our church choir should take tea at her home, after the funeral, which request & invitation was complied with..."[34]

Celebrations of one sort and another were often marked by the presentation of tea related gifts. Whether for birthdays, anniversaries, weddings, or as going away gifts, tea sets and accoutrements always pleased. Later generations would come to view such items as treasured heirlooms to be displayed and admired, until the time came to pass them on to the next generation. "...Today Aunt Bean was 61 years old. A number of us (relatives) paid her a visit this evening, 'surprized' her & presented her with a rocking-chair & a tea set. She was much pleased."[35]

Out of this age of growing prosperity came many of the things now referred to as "Victoriana." As the Queen's influence spread, she set styles and initiated traditions. People began trying to emulate her in all spheres of life. They admired her home life. They enjoyed the fact that she was obviously happily married. They observed and commented upon all that she did. They also watched her at tea.

A New Century

To make tea too strong is a sign of new friends.
If you make it too weak then you will lose friends.
ANONYMOUS

The turn of the century was to bring many changes. By far the most significant was the death of Queen Victoria in 1901. Her reign of more than sixty years had seen Canada grow from a pioneering nation to one of industry and commerce. Cities had grown, prosperity was increasing, and by 1902, when Edward VII and his beautiful wife Queen Alexandra were crowned, a new age of grandeur was dawning.

Under the influence of the new King and Queen, new trends and fashions were set. Edward's rather flamboyant style of life frequently attracted criticism. He was a womanizer and many of the values, which had become so deeply entrenched into society under Victoria, began to crumble.

The Edwardian period was therefore very different to that of the Victorian. Life took on a lighter flavour and a general sense of gaiety spread throughout the Empire. Such an atmosphere provided a grand setting for entertaining. Naturally, tea became even more fashionable and everybody who was anybody was sure to be seen enjoying five o'clock functions at the fashionable hotels of Britain, Europe and North America.

By this time Canadians were far more affluent than their parents had been. Happily, they also found themselves in a position to enjoy more leisure time. One of the developments which greatly affected the Canadian way of doing things was the expansion of the railway system. It was now possible to visit friends and family in other cities, in reasonable comfort and with relative ease. Business people were quick to assess the needs of the travelling public and, as had been done in Britain and in the rest of Europe, the construction of splendid and elegant railway hotels commenced.

Ontario's first grand railway hotel, the Château Laurier, was completed in 1912 in Ottawa. This gracious edifice at the foot of Parliament Hill was a huge success from the moment it opened its doors. Everyone was enthralled by it. Now the ambiance, and the elegance of taking tea at the Ritz, could be reflected in Canada's capital city. The railway hotels would build their reputations on elegance and comfort. They also provided ordinary people with a glimpse into the lifestyle of the wealthy. In splendid surroundings, common folk were able to rub shoulders with society folk.

This was a time when well-to-do young women were escorted hither and yon under the watchful gaze of chaperones. Naturally, many of them looked upon the whole business of being chaperoned as a rather tedious procedure. They must have, therefore, been delighted when the prospect of taking five o'clock tea at one of the swanky hotels arose. For such young women, this was one of the first things they were permitted to do without being accompanied by an ever-present body.

The hotels gradually became the focal points of their cities. Socialites flocked to them. Entertainers, politicians and royalty stayed in them. For ordinary people observing the rich and famous at these places became a pastime. And by the 1920's and 30's, everybody had acquired the habit of "taking tea."

Unlike the United States, tea was the preferred beverage in most Canadian homes. By now, tea drinking was almost as well established in Canada as it was in Britain. The serving of afternoon tea on a commercial level was in its heyday. It had become *the* thing to do. Wealthy women would hold lavishly arranged private tea parties in glamorous hotels. The hotels themselves began organizing all manner of special events around tea.

Not only was it possible to enjoy afternoon tea in a leisurely fashion, it was also possible to enjoy the glamour of "tea dances." Tea dances became and remained popular for many years, especially among the younger set who thronged to them by the hundreds on weekends. As they were not formal affairs, women usually wore ordinary afternoon frocks. Coats and gloves were laid aside. But hats, such an important part of a woman's wardrobe in this day, would remain on throughout.

The Rex Battle Trio were a popular attraction at afternoon teas served in the Palm Court, Royal York Hotel. *Royal York Hotel Archives*

Florence Grace Clement spent the winter months in Toronto. As an economic measure, once cool weather arrived, the family closed up their large home in Kitchener and moved into the Le Plaza Apartments. Florence adored city life and wrote of her activities in her diary. She was the daughter of a highly respected lawyer and also a cousin to Mr. A. Y. Jackson, who would later become one of Canada's most famous artists. In fact, it was the Clement family who provided cousin Alex with his first view of the Canadian Shield country when they invited him to their cottage at Portage Point near Honey Harbour in 1910. Florence often mentions the Jacksons in her diary, but on this occasion, Alex was missing: "Busted thro the work & had early dinner Dad & Mother went to the Movies & I went to see the Irish Players with the Williams met Pro & Pad Lewis & Esther, Mr. Wrong & Miss Nesmith for the Tea Dance at the King Edward. Went home to supper with Esther after"[36]

Tea dances generally ran between from four to six in the early evening. They were great fun. Young people sipped tea, munched on sandwiches and danced to the band. It was a grand way of meeting like-minded people. And naturally, it was a perfect place for mixing with the opposite sex.

There were, of course, many splendid hotels dotted throughout the province providing tea functions of one sort or another. In 1949 Barbara Ann Scott, Canada's famous Olympic skating star, was the guest of honour at a tea held at the Château Laurier, celebrating the anniversary of the Minto Skating Club, where she got her start.

Over steamy brews, romances have flourished, politicians have debated, wives have visited, school girls have chatted, grandmothers have bragged about little ones and business deals have been struck. Soon there were all manner of public places for taking tea. Department stores and better class restaurants provided afternoon tea havens for busy shoppers. During war-time when husbands were away and when food rations were enforced, the tea time ritual became more of a social occasion than ever before.

In private homes, afternoon tea had long been enjoyed. For country folk, the coming together over tea provided a much needed hour of socializing which went a long way toward relieving the isolation which encompassed the lives of many women. In towns, neighbours dropped in for tea. And along the way, children were also initiated into the rites of the tea ceremony, much as I had been.

By this time, many homes boasted elegant tea wagons. In March 1921, *The Victoria Colonist* ran a series of advertisements for "A neat tea wagon, in walnut finish, fitted with a moveable glass tray top and mounted on four rubber tired wheels". This description exactly fits the tea wagon my husband inherited from great aunts who lived in British Columbia at this time. No doubt hundreds of families purchased and enjoyed these elegant and useful items, and many tea parties were centred around them. When in use, the small side leaves of the tea wagon were opened to make a table. In the 1920's it was the fashion to cover the top with a small table cloth. Teapot, cups, saucers, sugar, cream, teaspoons and slop bowl were placed upon it. The lower level held plates and serviettes for passing round, as well as plates of fancy sandwiches, and cakes.

An alternative to the tea wagon would be one or two smaller tables. One for the tea pot and china and another for the muffin stand. This functional serving piece, made of wood, metal or wicker, was very much in vogue. Three or four levels of plates could be slotted, one above the other, to display afternoon tea food. Muffin servers were particularly prized because they allowed for an elegant display of food in limited quarters. Today they are making a great come-back.

As in the days of old, women still came together for mutual support. But by the mid 1900's many changes were taking place. Both World War I and World War II altered the lives of everyone. Women were entering the work force in greater numbers than ever before. There was less time and less demand for tea parties. One by one many of the establishments which had offered afternoon tea simply ceased serving it.

Three employees of the T. Eaton Co. store, Toronto, enjoy a tea break from the Eatonia tea wagon while stationed with the Canadian Army in Britain during World War II. Left to right: Highlr. A. Payton; Highlr. J. Grieveson; QMS D. Marr. *Eaton Collection, Archives of Ontario*

However, the demand for tea would shift to support for others, even during war-time. The changing work force certainly had an effect, but so too did advertising influences from the United States. Younger people found coffee to be more trendy than tea. Gradually there was a decrease in tea drinking. Happily, however, tea is on the march again.

We have travelled a long way since the days when people were exceptionally frugal by necessity. Certainly in pioneering times, anything beyond the odd meal, eaten at way-side inns when travelling, was unthinkable. We are fortunate to live in this age, surrounded by wonderful places to dine, to enjoy lunch or to savour the gracious experience of taking afternoon tea.

Tea Time

Stands the Church clock at ten to three?
And is there honey still for tea?
RUPERT BROOKE

Almost every village in Britain has at least one establishment offering teas, be it a café, farmhouse or elegant restaurant. On a typical afternoon drive, especially in country regions, one might pass as many as twenty such places. In this respect, many parts of Canada are beginning to resemble Britain. Most of our towns now have at least one afternoon tea establishment. Villages are also getting in on the act and many now boast splendid tea rooms. Tea rooms are flourishing and becoming too numerous to count. Even Bed and Breakfast establishments are beginning to offer teas. One wonderful thing about this variety of types of tea room is the splendid variation of edibles. Each establishment strives to create its own specialties and thereby puts a unique stamp on the occasion.

Traditionally there are three types of tea: "Cream Tea," "Afternoon Tea" and "High Tea." The Cream Tea is the simplest of teas, consisting of little more than a pot of tea and scone, served with homemade jam and heavy cream. If the host is being particularly generous, one might also receive an oatcake, muffin or perhaps a slice of plain tea bread. In Britain the cream accompanying scones is usually thick double cream or the famous clotted cream. Canadian tea establishments generally serve a domestic heavy cream or Devon cream imported from the United Kingdom. In some circumstances a mock clotted cream, made by beating together

37

whipping cream and a little sour cream with gelatin and a pinch of icing sugar, is served. The Cream Tea is the most common tea served in Canadian tea rooms. In fact there are many tea rooms which serve nothing but cream teas.

According to British tradition, Afternoon Tea is the elegant affair generally served between four and five o'clock. This is my favourite tea because I like the balance of the savoury and the sweet. Delicious morsels are often presented on three tier cake servers, allowing one tier for each course, so to speak. Afternoon Tea *must* include sandwiches. These are always served with crusts removed and assembled with a variety of fillings. Tasty meat or fish spreads have long been popular, as have smoked salmon and cream cheese concoctions. Tomato and cress are also prized, but the most famous of all is the cucumber sandwich. Next comes a selection of quite firm sweets, such as scones, which are always served with cream and jam. There might also be oatcakes, tea cakes and fruitcake and to top it all off, tiny fruit tarts, or similar pastries and small cakes or squares. For a truly sumptuous Afternoon Tea, seasonal fresh fruit, arranged in individual glasses, adds a finishing touch.

Afternoon Teas can be varied to suit the seasons. For instance, hot toasted tea cakes or crumpets make a marvellous beginning to a winter tea. Cucumber sandwiches are almost a prerequisite for a summer Afternoon Tea. The cucumber itself was rather slow in gaining in popularity. Samuel Johnson, who died in 1784, had a famous quote on the cucumber: "A cucumber should be well sliced, and dressed with pepper and vinegar, and then thrown out, as good for nothing."[37] In the late Victorian period, of course, cucumber sandwiches became synonymous with afternoon tea.

If one is intent upon serving an Afternoon Tea in a manner similar to that of one hundred years ago, the food ought to be such that it can be held in the hand without causing too much mess. This harkens back to a time when teas were served in drawing rooms or perhaps even outdoors during warm summer weather. Ladies invariably came to these affairs dressed in splendid outfits. Hats and gloves, which were everyday wear at this time, were not always removed prior to eating.

Summer-time tea party, River Bend, Waterloo. *Breithaupt-Hawetson-Clark Collection, University of Waterloo Archives*

High Tea is traditionally the evening meal of the ordinary people. Served at six o'clock, this meal has nothing to do with grand Victorian drawing rooms. It always includes sliced meats such as ham, tongue, jellied veal and beef. Potted meats, fish or seafood also grace the High Tea table. In addition, there would be flans, meat pies, savoury pies, cooked eggs, greens, tomatoes and perhaps a selection of ready-made sandwiches. In farmhouse kitchens, such as that of my great Aunt Hannah, one would also expect to be served homemade bread, buns, butter and cheese. For "afters" or "pudding," as dessert is generally termed, there would be jellies and custard, trifle, sponge cake, scones with cream and preserves, fruitcake, poached or fresh fruit, tarts and gingerbread, along with many other possibilities. And of course, lashings of tea "to aid the digestion."

The British High Tea table is truly deserving of the title "groaning board." Sundays were the days for enjoying High Tea at my home. Mother began her preparations on Saturday mornings by making those things which needed to "set," such as trifles and custard. Potted meats and fish would also have been made ahead and stored in the pantry food safe, a small cupboard covered with a fine wire mesh, basically designed to keep out unwanted pests and to provide good air circulation, but which also made a very useful barrier to the fingers of curious children. Salad ingredients, vegetables, and eggs came fresh from my father's vegetable garden and his hen house.

Memories of helping mother prepare foods for tea when I was a child all seem to focus upon winter time. As with most British homes, ours was not centrally heated. We all hugged the fireside when frosts came and we tried not to dally in remote parts of the house where the damp cold clung to everything. Spreading butter was the chore I hated the most. It was always rock hard and my little hands were forever ripping holes in the bread. For some reason, possibly due to her years of experience, mother never had any trouble with this.

The name "High Tea" very likely derives from that of "High Table," which, in days of yore, meant a raised dining table at which the most important people of an assemblage were seated. Today's analogy, except in places such as the colleges of Oxford and Cambridge which continue the practice of faculty sitting higher than students, would be the head tables of wedding receptions, where bridal parties sit facing their guests. High Table feasts are, by definition, rather

Afternoon Tea is served by ladies in costumes as worn fifty years ago. Photograph taken on February 28, 1919, upon the occasion of Eaton's Golden Jubilee.
Eaton Collection, Archives of Ontario

sumptuous. And although in medieval times very few ordinary people would have had any direct dealings with High
Table, they all knew what went on at the local manor house
when the Lord and Lady were entertaining. High Table became synonymous, in the minds of ordinary people, with
abundance. An abundant tea, served at the dining table,
therefore became known as High Tea.

One always sits at the table for high tea—it wouldn't be
High Tea otherwise. The reason for this is obvious. There is
simply far too much food for balancing acts with plates and
teacups. When Charlotte Brontë wrote *Shirley* in 1849, she
made a point of explaining that Yorkshire people took their
tea round the table. Then, as today, it was necessary to have a
multitude of plates to accommodate the abundance of food.

The elegance of an afternoon tea is not usually mirrored
in High Tea. In the north of England, it is more of a "sit th'
sel' down lass an' get stuck in" sort of affair. Dainty afternoon
tea sandwiches would never appear. This is a substantial

meal, often providing a party-like atmosphere of fun and laughter. The kettle is kept gently simmering on the hob, thereby ensuring an endless supply of fresh piping hot tea. High Tea was meant to be tucked into with great gusto.

About Tea

Of Heaven's many gifts to man,
And myraids thou they be,
There's none so all divinely great
As thou, oh wondrous Tea.

WILLIAM H. SEYLER

After lying dormant all winter, leaves of the tea bush, otherwise known as "Thea Sinensis", begin to sprout in the spring. Tea only grows at high altitude, no lower than 1000 feet above sea level and no higher than 7,000 feet. Intense cold would damage the plants. Except in those areas of Africa and India where tea is grown on lands flat enough to allow machinery to pick, tea is harvested by hand. Whether the end result is black or green tea, all tea leaves are green when picked. Black tea is produced by spreading the leaves out to wither. They are gently rolled, a process which breaks them up, releasing enzymes which cause the leaves to change colour. Within a few hours the leaves will have turned an orange-brown colour and the fermentation process has begun. Drying must begin at just the right moment to prevent over-fermentation. The leaves are rolled into a tight twist as they are dried. Green tea does not lie out to wither, nor is it allowed to ferment. As soon as it is picked, China Green tea is rolled and dried, sometimes by heating it in large woks over open fires. The Japanese Green tea is first steamed and then rolled and dried.

The Chinese have enjoyed tea for centuries, but the India tea trade did not begin until the mid 1800's. By this time the tea habit had become so intense that new tea sources had to be developed. To remedy this, the British set about looking for new lands suitable for cultivating tea gardens. They turned to India, to the lands they had previously cleared in order to grow opium, a substance which had proved so popular that even the gentlest of folks were inclined to look to it as a "cure-all" for all manner of complaints. Opium had been used also by the British as a trading commodity with the Chinese. Tea was exchanged for opium, hardly a commendable approach. However, because of political, moral and economic pressures, the business of growing opium was quickly surpassed by that of growing tea. The day of the India Tea Garden had come. Later, Ceylon (Sri Lanka), which had been primarily a region of coffee growing, began switching to tea. By the turn of the century, it too had developed healthy export markets.

Africa tea production also was begun in the early 1900's. The tea-gardens of Kenya have always produced a strong tea. These teas can be purchased in Canada, but are most often used to add bulk when blending. Tea from Argentina is imported into Canada as well. They are not sold as single teas, and are mostly used by manufacturers, particularly in the production of ice tea blends found on store shelves.

It did not take long before the stronger Assam and the flavourful Darjeeling teas of India gained favour in the western world. Because of soil and climatic conditions being different from those of China and Japan, these teas contain higher caffeine levels. They are also fermented to become blacker, resulting in a beverage with more "punch."

Naturally the teas that were popular in Britain soon were being exported to the colonies where they were greeted with equal approval. Black teas gained so much in popularity that before the century was out, green teas were being viewed with suspicion. "Beware of green tea, it is the unripe leaf and bears the same relation to the real article that the green does to the ripe peach," the *New Galt Cook Book* advised its readers.[38]

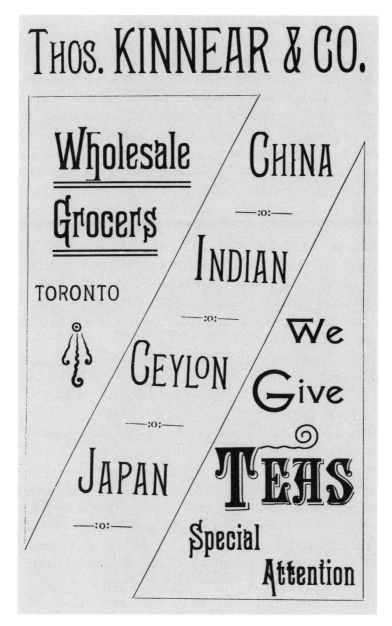

Advertisement taken from *A Sketch of the Growth and History of Tea and the Science of Blending Particularly Adapted to the Canadian Trade.* University of Waterloo Archives

In an age when tea was not obtained so easily, there was always concern about the quality. Everybody wanted a first-rate product. It was suggested that the best way to judge the tea was to place samples upon a piece of tea paper, breathe deeply upon them and then apply the nose, taking long inhalations. Women of long ago knew that a good tea should have a rich, sweet, aromatic odour, an inferior product would smell musty. Fresh tea was said to be as necessary to a successful tea trade as fresh butter to a successful butter trade. Therefore, no wholesaler or retailer was supposed to keep a pound of tea in his stock for more than four months. Disgruntled customers were often heard to complain that, with some merchants, it was the fashion to keep it for years. Tea will, of course, keep indefinitely if stored correctly—that is, in an airtight container, at room temperature and away from light. Exceptions to this are those teas flavoured with oils, such as the Earl Grey blend or those which include spices. They should be used within six months.

Tea blending recipes from the 1800's frequently refer to teas we seldom hear about today: Moning, Saryune Kaisow, Ning Chow Moning, Penyong Kaisow and Pecco Congou Kaisow. For tea blenders to produce a perfect blend for their clientele, it was often necessary to take the quality of water in their districts into consideration.

The flavour of local water was very much taken into account when Mr. Hugh Cooke, of Cooke's Old World Shop at Kingston produced what would become this company's famous "Garden Island" blend. In the 1930's, Mrs. D.D. Calvin had commissioned a blend of tea which would suit the hard water at her Garden Island home. Mr. Cooke produced for her a slightly smokey flavoured tea which infuses beautifully with hard water. Before long, relatives and guests to Mrs. Calvin's tea parties began purchasing the Garden Island tea for their own use.

Many of the tea blends available today were commissioned by wealthy individuals. One of the most famous examples of this is the very popular Earl Grey tea. Legend tells that during the Earl's tenure as Prime Minister of Britain, a British envoy saved the life of an important Chinese person. As a gesture of appreciation, the Earl received a package of tea. He enjoyed the flavour so much that he commissioned one of the tea companies to produce it for him. Mr. Sam Twining, of the Twining Tea Company, says that although this blend was unquestionably made up by his ancestors and the Earl, nobody bothered to register it. "As a result it has become a generic."[39]

Blends of tea have a way of coming into and going out of fashion. For example, "Lady Londonderry," a rather elegant and popular tea, was produced by Jackson's of Piccadilly for the famous English hostess, Lady Londonderry, during the early part of this century. In flavour, it was rather similar to the present day English Breakfast tea. Unfortunately, it was discontinued some years ago.

Tea is one of those products which has been loved and loathed at various times. After falling out of favour in the late 1800's, green tea was slow to regain respectability. As late as 1910, Canadians searching for "good tea" still were being advised to buy black tea. Abuse of tea was considered to be common. Tea also was blamed as a fertile source of nervous disease. And the habit of giving tea to young children was considered to be little short of criminal.

Today's society is very much focused on health issues. Consequently we are bombarded daily with information about what we should and should not drink and eat. When people in the medical profession publish results of studies on these matters, attitudes evolve. So, instead of "beware of green tea," as Victorian wisdom sometimes suggested, we now tout its beneficial properties. As well, black tea is viewed favourably these days. A growing body from the field of medicine suggest that all tea may impact positively upon the cardiovascular system. Other researchers continue to study tea as a cancer inhibitor.

Caffeine intake is certainly a concern for some people. According to Tea Council of Canada statistics, based upon average strength brews, a six ounce serving of brewed tea contains thirty-four milligrams of caffeine. The same amount of coffee contains ninety-nine milligrams. Obviously, the weaker the brew, the less caffeine. Those who prefer decaffeinated teas may purchase them in loose or in tea bag form. Some tea producers use methylene chloride to leech out the caffeine, others use ethyl acetate. The Metropolitan Tea Company uses a carbon dioxide gas for this purpose.

For the real purist, "organic" teas are available. Producers, ever vigilant regarding customers wants and needs, have set aside lands for growing these crops. These teas are priced slightly higher than regular teas to make up for less production per acre. They are claimed to be grown without artificial fertilizers, pesticides or herbicides.

In terms of value for money in beverages, tea tops the list. It is estimated that one pound of breakfast tea will produce about two-hundred and forty cups of tea. If you drink flavoured tea, you will get many more cups per pound. I encourage people to try as many teas as possible. If the tea selection in your area is rather limited, it is a very simple matter to order by mail, or by telephone, from one of the tea suppliers listed at the end of this publication.

If you are new to the pleasures of tea drinking, begin by purchasing small amounts of some of the more popular light tasting teas, such as Orange Pekoe, Darjeeling or Ceylon. Those who feel a little more adventurous might be interesting in trying an assortment of teas in "one taste only" sizes. Since tea drinking is such a delightful practice, why not give your palate a treat?

Brewing the Perfect Pot of Tea

Pour, varlet, pour the water,
The water steaming hot!
A spoonful for each man of us,
Another for the pot!
BARRY PAIN

It is not difficult to brew a perfect cup of tea. However, there are certain fundamentals which must be observed. First, the kettle should be filled with fresh running cold water and brought to a boil, while the teapot should be warmed by filling it with hot water. As the kettle approaches the boiling point, drain the water out of the tea pot and place the required amount of loose tea into it. Generally, one to three teaspoons are needed depending upon the size of pot and the degree of strength required. If desired, put the tea into a tea infuser. Pour rapidly boiling water over the tea and brew for three to five minutes. The ultimate anticipated quality will not result if the boiling water is allowed to cool by hitting a cold teapot. As well, a tea cozy is useful for keeping the tea nice and hot.

Since tea leaves need room to unfold during the brewing process, it is important not to pack infusers too tightly. The advantage of an infuser is that it allows the removal of the tea leaves from the pot, once the tea is brewed. If left in for too long, tannin is released, imparting a bitterness to the tea. If desired, tea leaves may be placed directly into the pot and the tea served with the use of a strainer. Give the tea a good stir prior to serving.

There is some debate as to the best type of teapot to use. At one time it was the fashion to brew tea in an earthen pot and then transfer it to a silver pot for serving. Purists still contend that metal teapots impart a metallic quality to the beverage. Generally, earthenwear, porcelain or china teapots are considered the best. During Victorian times, it was common for tea to be brewed in tin tea-steepers and later poured into and served from tea urns. As today, many Victorians recommended using earthen teapots since they thought the delicate leaf of tea should never touch metal.

In the very early Victorian period there were certain customs related to drinking tea. A spoon placed into the cup showed that no more tea was desired. Turning the cup over in the saucer implied the same. Another custom, which we might view as rather rude today, was to taste the tea from a spoon, following which action the hostess would question whether or not the tea was agreeable.[40]

Besides regular tea, the serving of Russian tea was popular, with lemon of course. In hot weather, it was recommended that people drink hot tea as a method of cooling down, but for special occasions, iced tea or punches made from tea were also served. Some early samples are as follows:

Russian Tea Mix

8 oz. Formosa Oolong
6 oz. Ceylon
2 oz English Breakfast tea
Dried peel of 1 orange cut into bits

Place 4 teaspoons of the above mix into the warmed teapot; scald with one quart of freshly boiling water.

Place in each cup:
1/2 tsp. of sugar-crystals
1/2 tsp. Jamaica rum
1/2 slice lemon
1 preserved cherry or strawberry

Iced-Tea Punch

6 tsp. tea (same mix as with Russian tea)
1 pt. freshly boiling water

Brew the tea in a normal fashion and let cool. When cold, pour into a jug containing the following:

1/2 cup granulated sugar
6 tbsps. lemon-juice
1 lemon
1 orange, sliced
1 qt. fresh strawberries,
2 cups pounded ice;

Add one bunch of fresh mint dusted with powdered sugar. When ready to serve, add one pint of carbonated water, Apollinaris or champagne.[41]

Cookbooks from the Victorian period tell much about the manner in which tea was brewed and served. Servants' manuals, which were very important to the training of servants, also provide a great deal of information. One of the most famous of these manuals is *The Finchley Manual of Industry*. Within its pages are to be found instruction in all matters pertaining to the duties of servants. Under the "tea-party" heading we find the following discourse:

"Q. We shall have a few friends to tea to-morrow evening, in a plain way; can you wait upon them handily?
A. Yes, Ma'am, I think I can; and I shall be very glad to try.
Q. You will be particular in making yourself neat and respectable in your dress?
A. Yes, Ma'am.
Q. Well, you know how to manage the urn and to place the teapot, and to make coffee, and to cut the bread-and-butter, and to prepare the toast, muffins, or whatever there may be?

A. Yes, Ma'am.

Q. Well, how do you commence?

A. If there are not more than three or four persons, ma'am, one large waiter will be sufficient to hold the cups of tea and coffee, placed alternately—the sugar and cream—and the bread-and-butter and toast.

Q. How do you carry your tray or waiter round to the company?

A. I hold it sufficiently low and near for the ladies and gentlemen to reach it easily.

Q. And how will you know whom to serve first?

A. Unless you tell me particularly, Ma'am, I shall serve the older ladies before the younger ones—all the ladies before any of the gentlemen—and the elder gentlemen before the younger ones.

Q. And you will watch when the cups are empty, that you may receive them on the waiter, and hand them back to me?

A. Yes, Ma'am.

Q. Should the company be more numerous than you seem to expect, what would you do?

A. Then I must have two waiters, Ma'am. one for the tea, coffee, sugar and cream; the other, for the bread-and-butter, toast, cakes or whatever there may be.

Q. And which do you hand first?

A. The tea and coffee Ma'am; and I must have a cup of each to offer to every person; and I must not hand the bread-and-butter and toast tray to any one who may not be supplied with tea and coffee."[42]

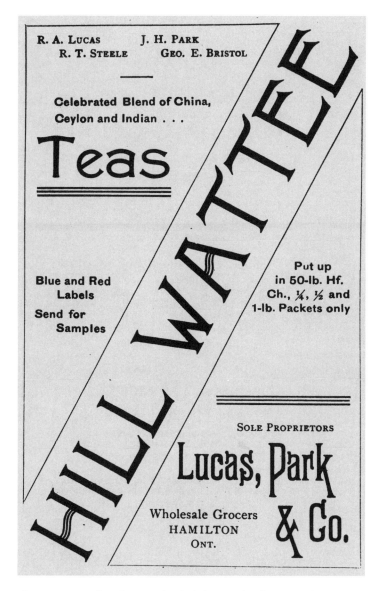

Advertisement taken from *A Sketch of the Growth and History of Tea and the Science of Blending Particularly Adapted to the Canadian Trade. University of Waterloo Archives*

Steel, Hayter & Co.

IMPORTERS OF

Indian Teas

Direct from their Estates in Assam.

❉

Assams, Kangras, Darjeelings, Indian Greens and CEYLON TEAS in stock.

❉

Proprietors of the well-known

"MONSOON" BRAND

Of Pure Unblended Indian Tea

IN THREE QUALITIES

FINEST ASSAM PEKOE

ASSAM BROKEN PEKOE

ASSAM PEKOE SOUCHONG

Packed in cases of 60 1-lb. caddies, or 12 5-lb. tins.

MESSRS. STEEL, HAYTER & CO. invite purchasers to send for samples and quotations, and to purchase their Teas direct from the Grower.

11 and 13 Front St. E., Toronto

London and Calcutta firm :
OCTAVIUS STEEL & CO.

Advertisement taken from *A Sketch of the Growth and History of Tea and the Science of Blending Particularly Adapted to the Canadian Trade. University of Waterloo Archives*

Teas in My Pantry

The cosy fire is bright and gay,
The merry kettle boils away
And hums a cheerful song
I sing the saucer and the cup;
Pray, Mary, fill the teapot up,
And do not make it strong.

BARRY PAIN

As in many homes, the old refrain, "let's have a nice cup of tea," rang throughout our house whenever there was a hint of frazzled nerves. It was clearly understood by everyone, young children included, that making a pot of tea was the first thing to do when the world needed "putting right." It was also the right thing to do when the world was bright and rosy. Since the habits we acquired when we are young tend to remain, it is not surprising that my kettle is constantly on the go.

In the old days, it was necessary for the mistress of the house to take sole charge of the key to the tea caddy in order to ensure that unscrupulous members of her household, or servants, did not pilfer the precious tea supply. The caddies were often made of wood and had two or three compartments. One side for green tea, the other for black, and a centre spot for mixing. In some cases, sugar was also stored in the tea caddy. Today, few people are lucky enough to own elaborate old fashioned caddies, but tea will store just as well in any air tight container. Blending of tea can be done in a mixing bowl.

Advertisement taken from *A Sketch of the Growth and History of Tea and the Science of Blending Particularly Adapted to the Canadian Trade. University of Waterloo Archives*

An abundance of specialty shops ensures that keeping our pantries well stocked with tea is a relatively simple matter. Literally there are hundreds of teas to choose from: single teas, blends, flavoured and herbals. The debate over which is better, loose tea or tea bags, will continue endlessly. Tea bags began when Thomas Sullivan, a New York tea and coffee merchant, packed loose tea in silk bags as tea samples in 1904. By 1952 the Lipton Company developed a four-sided bag to enhance the brewing process. Upon occasion I do use tea bags, especially when I am in a hurry, but I prefer to use loose tea and consider it to be a far superior product. Besides enjoying a finer flavour, although I am far from an expert, I get a great deal of pleasure out of experimenting with the blending together of various teas.

As indicated it is most important to store tea in air-tight containers. Never put tea in the fridge. It will keep nicely stored at room temperature in your kitchen cupboard or pantry. Do keep flavoured teas apart from regular teas to avoid contamination. Unless one deliberately blends Keemun with Earl Grey, for example, Keemun should not taste of bergamot.

The beauty of loose teas is that they can be blended to create just the right flavour. Of course, the notion of having to become an expert tea blender in order to enjoy a good cup of tea is just as ridiculous as the idea of having to acquire the musical skills of Pavarotti in order to enjoy a good opera. However, some experimentation is worth trying. Tea is, after all, a very personal drink.

Although my parents never wavered from their favourite blend, I choose to enjoy a wide range of teas and am always eager to try something new. In truth, tea-drinkers can become just as excited as wine-drinkers, given the prospect of securing an ounce or two of rare and exquisite tea.

The following is a list of teas which I always have on hand. In addition to these, I usually have an array of specialty blends.

China Teas

Keemun is a very flavourful black tea. Lightly brewed, it is thought by some to have the fragrance of an orchid. It can be served plain or with milk or lemon. Along with Darjeeling and oil of Bergamot, Keemun is often used in making the Earl Grey blend.

Lapsang Souchong should not be brewed too strongly and should never be served with milk. Legend suggests that discarded fishing nets once served as drying tables for this tea, hence the fishy, smoky, flavour. Today the smokiness is added during the drying process. While this tea is not one of my particular favourites, I always have it on hand for those friends who, "simply cannot do without it." Do try it.

Jasmine is delicately scented with the jasmine flowers and has a distinctive and pleasing taste.

Gunpowder is my favourite of all the China teas. It was so named by early traders because it resembled the grayish pellets of gunpowder ammunition used for firing muskets. These small, hard, pellets of tea unfold into bright green leaves during the brewing process. This tea has the lowest caffeine level of all teas and a most delicious flavour. Nothing is better for combating summer-time thirsts, so brew up a large pot.

Formosa Oolong is a lovely bed-time drink. As with Gunpowder, the caffeine content is low. Its delicate bouquet imparts a lovely peachy quality. The Chinese often brew a strong Oolong and sweeten it with honey, but I prefer to take it weak. The very best Oolong comes from Taiwan, formerly Formosa.

Dragonwell produces a delicate, smooth tasting, golden yellow brew. Resembling gray-greenish chips of wood, it is transformed into delicate green-yellow leaves during brewing. Although it is rather expensive, I highly recommend this tea. It can be purchased in 1/2 ounce size from Murchies of Vancouver.

India Teas

Assam is grown in the Brahmaputra Valley region of North East India. It reached the British markets in the late 1840's and became one of the most popular teas in Britain. Assam is fermented blacker than China Black Tea. It is this tea which imparts strength to Irish Breakfast Tea. It has a strong, slightly malty taste.

Darjeeling is grown in the foothills of the Himalayas, just below the snow line where the climate and rainfall are perfect. Because it includes a large percentage of fresh new leaves when picked, the tea is slightly paler than Assam. It is renowned for its delicate and distinctive muscatel flavour. This tea is best lightly brewed.

Nilgiri, grown in Southern India and also in Sri Lanka, is the flavour component of Breakfast blends. The taste is bright and it produces a very smooth golden brew. It is excellent alone, or blended.

Ceylon Teas

Kenilworth is an estate tea which makes a smooth flavoured and rich coloured brew. All tea lovers must surely enjoy this tea.

Japan Teas

Sencha is a pan fried green tea and one of the most popular of the Japanese teas.

My Favourite Blends

Tea companies carefully guard their recipes for blending tea. This accounts for the variation of flavours from one company to another. Experiment by trying several versions of a particular blend. Canadian tea companies constantly are inventing new and interesting blends. For example, the Murchie Tea Company of Vancouver was recently commissioned to create a special blend upon the occasion of the Canadian Broadcasting Corporation's sixtieth anniversary. It is named "CBC Tea." A very famous and very early Murchie blend is "Queen Victoria." This was created especially for Queen Victoria on her visits to Balmoral Castle in Scotland. There are literally hundreds of blends to choose from. One of the more interesting ways to keep abreast of tea blends is to request catalogues and newsletters from the tea companies.

Earl Grey is a splendid afternoon tea, very popular in North America. Once the domain of aristocrats, its delicate and unique flavour has earned it a place on the shelves of almost every supermarket in the nation. I especially value this tea because the richness of flavour is still evident even in the weakest brew. As with all blends, the flavour will vary from one manufacturer to another.

Russian Caravan is a blend of Keemun, Lapsang, Jasmine, Black Dragon (Oolong), and Gunpowder. A sip of this tea never fails to invoke images of camel caravans from long ago. It took a journey of up to eighteen months to transport tea from China, across Russia and into Europe. The old Caravan tea was a black semi-fermented tea of remarkable flavour. Present day Russian Caravan blend is said to be almost identical in taste. It is truly wonderful.

The Garden Tea Party

*Nothing imparts a better sense of the benevolence of Mother Nature
than taking tea in a beautiful garden.*
ALICE ROSE KELLY

EGG SALAD AND WATERCRESS SANDWICHES
CUCUMBER SANDWICHES
SCONES WITH DEVON CREAM AND PRESERVES
FRUIT TARTS
LEMON BLOSSOM COOKIES

While garden tea parties need not always be enormously lavish occasions, they do provide the opportunity to entertain on a large scale. We have Queen Victoria to thank for more or less inventing the garden tea party. In the mid 1860's, she gave an outdoor tea for a group of diplomats, politicians and other professionals. It was a splendid affair, everybody agreed. In fact it was so successful that it became an annual event. Throughout the nation a guessing game developed. Who would be lucky enough to be invited? Of course, everyone wanted to be included, such was the power of this status symbol. With the exception of a few brief years during the Second World War, Royal garden parties have provided summer pleasure to thousands.

Today, it would be impossible for a private individual to attempt to organize an affair even remotely resembling the Queen's. At the zenith of this tea party tradition, a staff of over six-hundred was required to serve up hundreds of gallons of tea and to pass round sumptuous trays of dainties.

Garden Tea Party at Herb Fleury's, Richmond Hill, Ontario. *Hillary House, The Koffler Museum of Medicine*

The garden tea party also became a popular entertainment in Ontario. A grand setting for such occasions was provided at Government House, located at King Street West and Simcoe Street, Toronto, the home of early Lieutenant-Governors of Ontario. On the spacious terrace and manicured lawns, Toronto society folk, along with other prominent Canadians, were invited to rub shoulders and mingle with visiting Royalty and dignitaries. Under the capable direction of Thomas Lymer, who served as Butler and Chief Steward under eleven of Ontario's Lieutenant-Governors, many splendid garden tea parties were held.

Up to five hundred people would attend. And if the guest of honour was important enough, the afternoon function might be followed by a state dinner for eighty or more guests. Mr. Lymer's secret for success was "careful planning" and "consideration for the guests". One of his rules regarding tea parties was that food should not be sticky, nor too crumbly. It was important, he thought, that guests should feel as elegant at the close of the function as they had at the opening. ..."People who are holding a tea cup in their hands do not want a sticky cake that crumbles, they prefer the light firm sponge cakes and assorted sandwiches, mainly of chicken, tomatoes or cress."[43]

Two garden tea parties of particular interest had taken place in 1879. The guests of honour were Queen Victoria's daughter, Princess Louise, and her husband, John Campbell, Marquis of Lorne, who was appointed Canada's Governor-General in 1878. Tongues had long wagged about the Princess for her outspoken manner and difficult nature. But by this time, her husband's homosexuality was also feeding the rumour mill. Naturally, all Toronto society turned out to be part of this tea party. Everybody wanted to be able to say that they had seen this fascinating pair and had heard the latest gossip. Although the Lieutenant Governor, with his family and servants, had vacated Government House in order that the Lorne's might have a private stay, Mr. Lymer remained to oversee arrangements.

One of the most splendid Government House garden parties was that of 1901, when the Duke and Duchess of Cornwall and York, (later to become King George V and Queen Mary) visited. Refreshment tents were arranged on the lawn. The weather was perfect and a whole list of "who's who" in Ontario attended. It was a fabulous affair. A panoramic photograph, discovered in the Thomas Lymer Papers, is thought to document this event.

A Garden Party at Government House, Toronto, 1901. *Archives of Ontario*

Of course, most outdoor tea-parties were celebrated in a very different fashion. The afternoon tea at the bottom of the garden for instance, has long been a relaxing and favourite warm weather pastime of Canadian families. In fact, outdoor teas are suitable for just about any occasion. In late Victorian times, an informal outdoor tea might consist of dainty plates of small sandwiches, olives, fancy cakes, and bonbons and a pot of tea. For a more formal affair, bouillon, hot or cold, coffee, chocolate, Russian tea, or another favourite blend, iced tea punch, sandwiches, afternoon tea cakes, ices, frappés, or punches would be in order. Napkins were recommended as protection to the gloves and frocks.

A Winter Tea

It snowed last year too.
I made a snowman
and my brother knocked it down
and I knocked my brother down
and then we had tea...
DYLAN THOMAS

POTTED SHRIMP SERVED ON FINGERS OF TOAST
TOASTED TEA CAKES
GINGER AND TREACLE SCONES WITH RUM BUTTER
GRANNY'S DUNDEE CAKE

In some ways, winter teas are the most memorable. There is something especially delightful about snuggling up in front of a cozy fire with a well-ladened tea tray. My family's favourite winter tea is that of Christmas Eve. It is an occasion which has developed into a great tradition. Christmas preparations are always well in hand by this time and tea time marks the beginning of our Christmas festivities. At three o'-clock sharp, the kettle goes on. Warm toasty things, ginger scones, slices of fruitcake and a pot of our favourite brew are set on the tea tray. As tea is enjoyed, we listen to a recording of Dylan Thomas reciting *A Child's Christmas in Wales*.

Winter has always offered a grand opportunity for entertaining. On the 4th of January, 1900, Emma Breithaupt had fifty ladies in for tea to celebrate the New Year. Two weeks later Louis, her husband, wrote that they had a pleasant sleighing party to Galt. "Emma, Evelyn, Miss Beck, Mrs. (Harvey) Dewitt, Ed. Dewitt & I. Miss Wright & Mr. Ch. Hall took tea with us at the Queen's Hotel there. Great snow fall to-night."[44]

Boxing Day of 1911 was also marked by a visit "to Wm & Mattie's for 'high tea' & had a pleasant time."[45]

While the Breithaupt girls were home for school holiday, relaxation and pleasure were the order of the day. "Did not get up until late a.m. afraid. I am getting into bad habits here at home. Had a good steak dinner. Mamma and Edna went to Guelph for the afternoon. Rose, Lil & I went downtown and did a bit of shopping then, 'Toasted our shins' until tea time."[46]

Back at school, the fun continued. "Junior meeting after dinner. Ruth got a funny hat from her mother. The four of us went to Ross's for afternoon tea. Hadn't permission of course, but we had lots of fun."[47]

Another visit to the Ross's took on a rather different tone. "Lil took Jane & I to Presbyterian church. Mrs. Ross walked part way home with us and asked us for afternoon tea...At four o'clock Jane, Lil & I went down to Ross's. Disgraced ourselves by eating too much at Ross's."[48]

Whatever winter-time activities are planned, tea can become part of the affair. At our house, after ski teas are popular. So are snuggling by the fire with a good book teas — especially on cold blizzardy days. But best of all are those teas which include a gathering of friends.

A Children's Tea Party

Mommy set the table
Daddy brewed the tea
Teddy ate it all up
There was none for me
ALICE ROSE KELLY

DROP SCONES WITH BUTTER AND HONEY
PEANUT BUTTER AND JELLY SANDWICHES
EGG SALAD SANDWICHES
MINIATURE SCONES WITH CREAM AND PRESERVES
MINIATURE VICTORIA SANDWICH CAKE

Tea parties provide children with a magical way of learning table manners. It is quite amazing to see tiny tots switch into a "neat and tidy mode" once they sit down to a prettily arranged tea table. The dress-up part of tea parties offers great fun too. So does pretending to be a "big" person. And when pouring out their very own cups of tea becomes part of the game, children are totally enthralled.

Children of the Victorian era also enjoyed teas. However, there were different ideas in those days about which foods were suitable for young children. For instance, raisins and currants were thought to be too much for their digestive organs. Of all the cakes, the plain sponge cake was considered the most appropriate. Fruit cakes, or scones containing dried fruit, never would appear at a nursery tea. On the whole, they were fed rather plain fare with the odd jam tart thrown in for a treat.

Today of course, children are much more sophisticated

and enjoy an incredible range of foods. However, since all little ones have likes and dislikes, the food at tea time should be fairly basic. It is best to serve sandwiches with fillings the children are accustomed to. They can be made fancy by cutting them into shapes with a cookie or pastry cutters. Make small scones for children by cutting the dough with a small (2 inch) pastry cutter. Similarly, a small Victoria Sandwich Cake can be made by baking the batter in a small cake tin. I use a 5 1/2 x 2 1/2-inch cake tin which I fill three-quarters full with batter. Once the cake has baked and gone cold, I slice it horizontally, sandwiching the two pieces together with jam.

Whether children share an afternoon tea with a group of friends, or with a single teddy bear, they thrill to handle tiny cups, creamers and teapots. Miniature tea sets are great fun, but it is important that they contain handles which are adequate to allow the child to grip each item properly.

Joel Hoffman, Megan and Alex Gregor take tea. *Photo by George McDermott*

A very weak brew of regular tea works best since most of the fun comes from adding the milk and stirring. Herbal and flavoured teas or simply warmed fruit juice may also be served. As far as children are concerned, if it pours from a tea pot, it is tea.

Whether the children are part of a picnic tea on the lawn, or seated indoors at an elaborately arranged tea table, a tea party will present them with magical moments.

My Choice of Tea Rooms

*'There are few hours in life more agreeable than the hour
dedicated to the ceremony known
as afternoon tea.'*
HENRY JAMES

I have been "taking tea" in Canada for many years, Yet I
still find myself being pleasantly surprised by the degree of
variation among tea rooms. If we look hard enough we can
find all manner of places, to suit all tastes. For those who
yearn for magnificent splendour, tea at a luxurious hotel
might be in order. Some people are most comfortable taking
tea in the homey atmosphere of a bed and breakfast. Others
may search for built-in entertainment at places such as the
Russian Tea Room in Edmonton where customers may hire
psychics, or have their tea leaves read by those who claim to
"have the gift." I remember sitting in this tea room watching
customers going through the motions. Hushed voices floated
across the room. Dreams were enhanced or shattered, based
upon nothing more than the formation of tea leaves in the
bottom of tea cups. It brought to mind girlhood games of tea
leaf reading and of searching for symbols of romance and
wealth amongst the still damp leaves. It was enormous fun,
but even then we didn't take it seriously. Today, it is the un-
used tea leaf which interest me. Will it forecast a good brew?

The art of brewing a good cup of tea is very simple, yet so
many establishments—yes, even some of the more famous of
our tea rooms—are providing their customers with inferior
brews. The tea should come freshly brewed and piping hot.

The larger the selection of teas, the better. Since ordering tea from wholesalers is a relatively simple matter, there is little or no excuse for tea rooms not having a reasonable selection of teas. The primary consideration of a tea room ought to be quality of beverage. Unfortunately, there are many tea rooms whose proprietors seemingly have such a lack of interest in the tea they serve that choice is limited to one or two varieties of tea bags.

Regardless of where one goes for tea, one thing is very clear. Proprietors of first-rate tea rooms always have known that attention to fine detail pays dividends. It is the ability to set a truly welcoming and quality tea table that sets a good tea-room apart from others.

Afternoon Tea ought to contain all those elements which lend gentility to the occasion. It begins with delicate china and shining silver carefully arranged on immaculate linen. We add inviting food, exquisitely arranged, courteous attendants to replenish the tea-pot and special companions to share in the pleasure.

Tea Rooms, by definition, are establishments which prepare their own foods. Baking should be done on site and served fresh each day. Sandwiches must be prepared immediately prior to serving in order to ensure a moist freshness. Nobody enjoys soggy or dried out sandwiches. It is also most important that other ingredients, such as fruit and cream, are absolutely fresh. Naturally, the "last minute" nature of preparing a good afternoon tea implies extra effort on the part of the kitchen staff. Such effort really is worthwhile. It does not go unnoticed by the customer and, in the long run, will lead to increased business.

Currently we are witnessing a great revival in the institution of afternoon tea. Tea establishments are springing up all across the country. On the West Coast, the presence of a strong British element has ensured the continuance of this tradition. But in the East, possibly with the exception of large city hotels, afternoon tea was virtually unheard of until quite recently. Fortunately, for people such as myself, wee pockets of interest in afternoon tea could be found if one searched hard enough. For more than twenty years I have regularly taken tea at The Great British Emporium in New Dundee, Ontario. This establishment, which attracts a faithful clientele from among United Kingdom ex-patriots, must be one of the longest continuously operated tea rooms in the province.

Unfortunately, the term "tea room" is frequently being used by establishments which have no more to do with the serving of tea than a regular cafe or restaurant. Tea Room has become rather a trendy title. So, buyer beware! Do not take it for granted that you can march into any establishment operating under the name of Tea Room and expect to be provided with a good brew, or with a delicious afternoon tea.

A sampling of the extraordinary collection of tea pots found at The Mad River Tea House. *Linda Giffen, Creemore, Ontario*

A tea room which cannot be overlooked is The Mad River Tea House at Creemore, Ontario. Although it does not offer a traditional afternoon tea, this tiny little tea house is an intriguing place to visit. Sandwiches, soups and sweets accompany special "Mad River" blend teas and coffees. The little store, which can seat only nine people, is filled with all man-

71

ner of tea time necessities. For example, teapot collectors will be pleased to learn that there are over three hundred different teapots on display. On warm weather days, up to forty-two people can be served on the outside patio.

One of the joys of going out for tea is that the occasion can be as simple or as formal as we wish. In 1914, the Breithaupt girls discovered a new place which obviously suited them. "Up for breakfast—swept room etc. down to the Laundry to press shirt. Music lesson & practice. Whole bunch of us & Deit & I, Marg, Ruth, Marion B., Allie, Jean, Joe, Myrt, Dora etc. all went to New Tea Room. It is great."[49]

So, search out exactly the type of environment you most enjoy. Fortunately, we now have many places to choose from, each providing its own mood and specialty of the house.

Over the years and with much experience, I have developed my own personal preferences. What follows is a introduction to some of my favourite places to take tea in Ontario. Amongst this mix of hotels, tea rooms and bed and breakfast establishments you will find some which have been in the tea business for many years. Others are relatively new. In different ways, they all provide what I look for when going out for tea.

Now for the tea of our host,
Now for the rollicking bun,
Now for the muffin and toast,
Now for the Sally Lunn!
SIR WILLIAM SCHWENCK GILBERT

❀ ❀ ❀

Eagleview Manor
Nanny's Tea Room
ST. MARYS, ONTARIO

St. Marys, the "stone town" houses many other splendid homes, but the moment I entered Eagleview Manor, I knew I was in for a treat. This magnificent "Queen Anne" style house, built in 1905 by local contractor, William Hylands, contains exquisite detail. To begin with, there is a marvellous wide sweeping staircase, one that is the dream of every bride wishing to make a grand entrance. Most windows in the house contain wonderful stained glass. The dining room, also referred to as "Nanny's Tea Room," retains its original oak wainscotting. The second floor contains five spacious bedrooms, some of which are used to accommodate bed and breakfast guests. There is also an old fashioned "consumptive" porch, a reminder of the time when the hold on life was so tenuous because of diseases such as tuberculosis. Instead of accommodating convalescents, it now provides visitors with panoramic views of the town. This is a house which truly offers a glimpse into the elegance and grace which marked the Edwardian period.

A visit to St. Marys is always a treat. If you add Afternoon Tea at Eagleview Manor, you are guaranteed an excellent time. The hostess, Pat Young, serves a delightful tea consisting of an assortment of dainty tea sandwiches, plain and wholewheat scones served with cream and a selection of preserves and lemon curd. This is followed by a variety of tiny squares and fresh fruit salad. Teas are Earl Grey and Tetley. Flavoured and herbal teas are also available.

Great attention is paid to the table settings. Silver and crystal rest on hand embroidered table-cloths. Fresh roses and candles add a festive touch. The pretty afternoon tea china is a family heirloom and used with great pride. Everything at Eagleview Manor is fresh and pure. Groups of up to twenty can be accommodated and private tea parties to celebrate special occasions can be arranged.

There are so many wonderful things to do in St. Marys. Personally, I could spend a day just gazing at the splendid architecture. The town, famous for its limestone, contains the largest concentration of 19th century stone buildings in Ontario. There is interesting and pleasant shopping and delightful walks along the Thames River and Trout Creek. As well, the town boasts of their forty-five acres of parkland. The St. Marys Museum, located in a striking limestone house dating back to the 1850's, contains artifacts relevant to the history of St Marys, as well as genealogical and other information. There is also an Opera House, a Carnegie library and a splendid Town Hall which houses an upper level theatre. The Rt. Hon. Arthur Meighen, Prime Minister of Canada during the early 1920's, was born near St. Marys in 1874. A statue in his honour stands in Lind Park, and is worth a look on your next visit to St. Marys.

❊ ❊ ❊

Langdon Hall Country House Hotel
BLAIR, ONTARIO

Just outside the small village of Blair, which is now part of Cambridge, lies Ontario's answer to the stately homes of Britain. To do justice to the romance of a Langdon Hall experience, one really ought to arrive by horse and carriage. The scene opens with a long winding lane-way passing through dense Carolinian woods. Grandeur is apparent the instant this splendid Georgian country mansion comes into view. The hall was built in 1898 for Eugene Langdon Wilks, great-grandson of the fabulously wealthy New York business tycoon, John Jacob Astor. Mr. Wilks' first wife died childless. He then married Marguerite Briquet of Geneva, Switzerland. They had three daughters. The family lived alternately in Europe and at Langdon Hall, which remained in the family until

1982. Today, Langdon Hall Country House Hotel is part of the elite Relais & Châteaux Association, for which, "character, courtesy, charm, calm, and cuisine" are prerequisite.

I think of Langdon Hall as a place for all seasons and, since I am fortunate enough to live fairly close, I am able to visit frequently. Afternoon and Champagne teas, prepared to perfection by Chef Louise Duhamel, consist of assorted sandwiches, sultana and currant scones served with vanilla flavoured heavy cream and preserves, followed by spice and fruit cake and cookies of the day. Langdon Hall acquires the forty-two per cent heavy cream from a local dairy. Champagne teas include the addition of a glass of Mumm's Cuvee Napa and fresh seasonal berries and cream. Everything is arranged with exquisite taste and served by an attentive and well-trained staff.

Choices of tea are extensive. Standard blends include Earl Grey, English Breakfast, Queen's Blend and London 77. Single teas include Assam and Orange Pekoe. Chunmee, a popular green tea, is also offered. There is also a generous selection of flavoured and herbal teas. All are served as they ought to be, piping hot with close attention paid to customers' needs.

One of the marvellous things about Langdon Hall is its self-sufficiency. A large vegetable garden, managed by full-time staff, keeps the kitchen well stocked and ensures freshness and quality. This kitchen garden, with its marvellous old south-facing stone wall, is a must to see. Unless the grounds are buried under a blanket of winter snow, do take a walk around. For most of the year, flower beds provide an endless varieties of colour. These gardens, and a host of magnificent trees and shrubs, offer a splendid botanical feast.

Langdon Hall is a stone's throw from many of the wonderful attractions of Waterloo Region. Explore Scottish heritage, so evident in the architecture of downtown Galt, or take a trip to northern parts of the region where Mennonite farmers bring Mother Nature's bounty to country markets. Take time to discover this area, so rich in tradition and history.

❊ ❊ ❊

McGregor House
Victorian Tea Room and Treasures
SOUTHAMPTON, ONTARIO

The settling of Southampton began in 1848 when the first log house was erected. From this modest beginning a town of elegance would grow. Today, dotted throughout the laneways and by-ways of this community are many splendid Victorian properties. McGregor House is one of these gems.

I think of McGregor House as a very happy home. It was built in 1875 for the local shoemaker, Peter McGregor. One can almost feel the laughter of his eight children still ringing through the rooms. Today, instead of the fixing of hearty meals for a family of ten, the kitchen is given over to the preparation of lunches and afternoon teas, which are greatly relished by those lucky enough to have discovered this treasure. The house, located on a quiet lane, is far enough removed from the sounds of town life to offer a peaceful and tranquil respite. Lake Huron is only one block away.

McGregor House is owned and operated as a bed and breakfast by Anne and Jan Riddall. Anne's English heritage contributes greatly to her enjoyment of, as well as her expertise in, the afternoon tea experience. The tea room is adorned with tea time treasures. Exquisite tea pots and china sit ready for use in an open cupboard. Family heirlooms, such as Great Granny's lace work, adorn the walls. Everywhere there is an atmosphere of peace and graciousness. The Riddall's say: "When we walked in the front door, we knew it was the house for us. Owning an English tea room was our dream, and this heritage home seemed to have the perfect ambiance and set-up."

Anne and Jan have a great interest in tea. Their stock is generous and is brewed to perfection. Among others, they serve Darjeeling, Nilgiri, Assam and green teas from Japan and India. In addition to their own blend, "McGregor House

Tea," they also serve a large variety of flavoured and herbal teas.

The Afternoon Tea consists of a delicious and generous supply of very attractive sandwiches, followed by scones with Devon cream, preserves and home-made lemon curd. This is followed by a selection of fruit tarts, cookies and tea bread, decorated with tidbits of fresh fruit. In addition to Afternoon Tea, traditional cream teas and children's teas are offered. The Riddall's relaxed and welcoming manner will ensure that folks return, again and again. A visit here is a fabulous treat!

There is much to be seen around the town of Southampton, which claims to be the "Oldest Port on the Bruce Coast." Naturally, it boasts a proud history and marine heritage. You might begin the day by exploring the quaint laneways, searching out some of the fine shops. Then, work up a healthy appetite for afternoon tea by visiting the Bruce County Museum, or try a trip around the Art School and Gallery. And, if that has not done the trick, a brisk walk along the beach will ensure that justice is done to one of Anne's delicious spreads.

※ ※ ※

Mrs. Carter's Tea Room
STRATFORD, ONTARIO

Mrs. Carter's is one of Stratford's newest businesses. It is a charming little tea room conveniently located right in the city centre. Formerly a furniture store, this is just the type of place we all dream of finding, especially after a few hours of tripping about when that old familiar "gasping for a cup of tea" stage swiftly approaches. Wingback chairs along with an inviting fireplace and attractively set tables do much to create a homey environment. There is also a deliciously old fashioned quality about this tea room, which for me is reminiscent of many British tea rooms.

Tea time at Mrs. Carter's offers a full afternoon tea with a selection of tea sandwiches, scones with Devon cream, preserves and sweets. Cream teas, such as the "Carter Tea for Two", or simply "Scone and Tea," are also available. Mrs. Carter's tea selection is excellent. Loose teas include Earl Grey, Prince of Wales, Decaffeinated, English Breakfast, Irish Breakfast, Tarajulie, Mim and Lucky Dragon. Also there is a large selection of flavoured and herbal teas.

This is one of those wonderful establishments which also contains a bakeshop. The moment the first whiff of goodies is detected you will be hooked. A wide variety of tea and tea related articles can also be purchased in the gift shop. In all, Mrs. Carter's is a perfect place to spend a couple of hours. The whole idea is for customers to enjoy sitting around the cozy fireplace, perhaps with a magazine or book, or to enjoy conversation and food in an atmosphere of calm relaxation. Lunch is served daily, with dinner available on Fridays.

There is another side to this business. Duggan Place is a large Victorian home built in 1891 for one of Stratford's prominent merchants, Jeremiah Duggan who became quite famous by establising the largest department store west of Toronto. Here the Carter family operates a bed and breakfast. They, along with three other similar establishments, offer "Bed and Breakfast Getaways" planned around interesting themes. One of these events revolves around Mrs. Carter's Tea Room. Guests will gather around the fireplace and listen to Mary Eileen McClear unfold the mystique and art of storytelling. What a fabulous way to spent a blustery weekend in March!

Stratford is a picturesque city. Exploring it could keep you busy for days. Although most famous for Shakespearean Festival Theatre, there are also many other wonderful attractions. Try boating on the Avon, or perhaps take a double decker bus tour around the city. For history buffs, the Perth County Archives is located here. There are also historical walking tours—an excellent way of working up an appetite. And, the shopping is terrific.

❄ ❄ ❄

Queenston Heights Restaurant
QUEENSTON HEIGHTS, ONTARIO

The Queenston area is one of Ontario's special treasures. I stumbled upon afternoon tea here quite by accident in the early 1980's. What a treat it was! In our family, prior to this event, Queenston was famous for two reasons. The Battle of Queenston Heights and the little garage which kept us supplied with spare parts for the clunkity old Land Rover in which we trundled around Ontario. I recall that it was with a view to rewarding my patience during a "spare parts" trip that Peter suggested we visit the restaurant up on the Heights. I was rewarded exceptionally well!

First of all, the restaurant is set amongst magnificent scenery. We have come to expect high standards in floral splendour from the Niagara Region. The landscaping here will not disappoint. Although closed during winter months, I particularly make a point of taking tea at Queenston during the early Spring. I know that when my garden is still hidden under half frozen soil, the benevolent climate in these parts will offer a wonderful array of colour.

From high atop Queenston Heights, views from the restaurant windows are incredible. A carpet of greenery sweeping all the way down to the banks of the Niagara River offers a marvellous panorama. Inside the restaurant, the service is formal, with perfect table settings. There is no doubt that the staff at this restaurant know how to serve a splendid afternoon tea.

The tea, done to perfection by Chef Herbert Baur, begins with cucumber, salmon salad, and cheese and carrot sandwiches, followed by Nova Scotia blueberry scones with butter, cream and preserves. To top everything off, chocolate eclairs, fancy cookies and the famous Queenston Heights Restaurant farmhouse fruit loaf. English Tea Time, Earl Grey, Darjeeling, along with flavoured and herbal teas, are available.

One of the famous novelties at the Queenston Heights Restaurant is its flavoured butter. This was the brain child of manager, Carol Muscato, and adds a special touch to afternoon tea.

There are many attractions in this region. The Laura Secord House, located right in the village of Queenston, provides a marvellous glimpse into early life in this part of the province. Scenic drives along the Niagara Parkway offers beautiful scenery. Wineries, fruit markets, historic points of interest and hiking trails are all part of the pleasures of exploring this area.

❊ ❊ ❊

Silkweeds
Petticoat Parlour Victorian Tea Room
ST. GEORGE, ONTARIO

The highlight of a day in St. George for me is slipping into the world of "Victoriana," courtesy of Silkweeds and Petticoat Parlour. This delightful property, built as a residence in 1880, is a true Victorian home. Today, as visitors wander through the beautifully decorated building, "theme" rooms filled with all sorts of interesting merchandise bring pleasant surprises. The building houses a total of six rooms of merchandise. During weekends, a hostess in period costume greets visitors at the door. Hospitality is one of the main concerns here. It does not take long to realize that it is one of those places in which one immediately feels at home. The little touches of home life cleverly dotted throughout the rooms may have something to do with this. The overall ambiance of this establishment provides a sense of family life in days gone by.

Petticoat Parlour Victorian Tea Room is located on the main floor. Here, while listening to the muted sounds of classical music, a delightful afternoon tea can be enjoyed. The tea room is tastefully appointed and tea is served with only the finest accoutrements. Edibles consist of finger sandwiches, freshly baked scones with currants, homemade preserves and cream, as well as sweet treats such as shortbread, squares and pastries. Everything is beautifully presented on fine china servers. There is no doubt that this tea room is certain to develop an enviable reputation among the tea rooms of Ontario. There is a splendid emphasis upon high quality teas at this establishment. Presented under the McKee label, one of Ontario's suppliers of tea, the offerings include: Keemun, Jasmine, English Breakfast and Earl Grey. A large selection of flavoured and fruit blend teas is also offered. Tea and useful accoutrements are also sold in the gift shop.

For those who like nothing better than scouting around antique stores, the town of St. George is a little paradise. Each June people travel from far and wide to enjoy the annual antique show. St. George also provides an opportunity to explore other aspects of the heritage of South Dumfries Township. The Adelaide Hunter Hoodless Homestead, home of Adelaide Hunter Hoodless, founder of the Women's Institute, is located on the western outskirts of St. George. Open from late February until mid December, this fascinating place offers a glimpse into homestead life from the period of 1857 to 1910. Still others come to St. George for the annual Lily show held each July. The Apple Harvest is a September attraction, while December offers a host of Yuletide festivities. The main street of St. George boasts a splendid Victorian Inn as well as many interesting stores.

※　※　※

The Château Laurier
Zoé's
OTTAWA, ONTARIO

I have always adored Ottawa, with its commanding architecture, buildings dripping with history, wonderful blend of French and English culture and scenic beauty which is around every corner. Who can resist the walk down Parliament Hill to the Château?

I was first introduced to tea at Zoé's on a cold winter's day. It was two weeks before Christmas. All of my Yuletide preparations had been completed, and a few days of work and relaxation in the city had came my way. There was something quite marvellous about gazing through frost flecked windows onto frigid December streets. I remember watching people scurrying by, mostly with the look of "determined Christmas shopper" stamped upon their faces. Snug inside Zoé's, I had entered a completely different world. I was enjoying a fabulous afternoon tea. Immediately I fell in love with the place and have returned, again and again.

The Château was the brainchild of Charles Melville Hays, an American-born General Manager of the Grand Trunk Railway of Canada. He commissioned work on the hotel as well as an adjacent railway station. However, shortly before the hotel was due to open, tragedy struck. In the wee hours of 15 April 1912, Mr. Hays was amongst those who perished when the *Titanic* sank during her maiden voyage. Hays and his family were returning to Canada, bringing furniture specially designed for his new hotel. Replicas can be found in the Château Laurier today. He never saw his dream fulfilled. The official opening of the hotel was postponed until 1 June 1912, when former Prime Minister, Sir Wilfrid Laurier, officiated in place of Mr. Hays.

Despite the tragic beginning, the hotel became an immediate success. Tea time soon became an integral part of the hotel's features In the early 1920's, people met in the long hallway called Peacock Alley, where, to the strains of a live orchestra, delightful afternoon teas were served. Later, tea was served in the Jasper Tea Room, famous for its striking interior decor. The pegged oak dance floor, surrounded by a series of columns carved into totem poles, was the scene of many a fine tea dance.

Today, this location is Zoé's, named for Zoé Lafontaine, wife of Sir Wilfrid Laurier. Here we find the perfect setting for tea. There really is nothing nicer than taking a mid-afternoon break and scooting down to the Château for tea. The

Château Laurier, Ottawa

food is simply splendid. To begin with, there are sandwiches made of cucumber and cream cheese, smoked turkey with raspberry mayonnaise, and salmon and dill herb, followed by Victoria scones with cream, homemade marmalade and strawberry jam. Then there are seasonal fruit tartelettes and afternoon tea cake exquisitely prepared by Executive Chef Patissier, Ernst Frehner. A Teddy Bear's Tea party is held each December to which tiny tots bring pet bears. Fashion show teas are another feature of Zoé's. Tea choices include: Earl Grey, Orange Pekoe, Irish Breakfast, Lapsang Souchong, Darjeeling, Jasmine and a selection of herbal teas.

Zoé's is a good place for celebrity watchers, Sir Peter Ustinoff took tea here. Other well-knowns include Yousuf Karsh the famous photographer, Roger Moore who is perhaps best known for his James Bond role, Bryan Adams, Paul Newman and Joanne Woodward, to name but a few.

The list of attractions in Ottawa is endless and therefore impossible to do justice to in this short space. However, outdoor attractions are planned on a year-round basis. Besides spectacular architecture such as the Parliament buildings, there are wonderful theatres, museums, shops and restaurants.

❈   ❈   ❈

The Doctor's House
KLEINBURG, ONTARIO

A breathtakingly beautiful landscape sets the scene for the charming village of Kleinburg. For me, a visit here is a treat under any circumstances. The village was established in 1848 by John Nicholson Kleine who lent his name to the settlement. He also became quite famous for building the largest sawmill between Toronto and Barrie. The fine legacy of these early lumbering days is still evident in the village's splendid architecture.

By 1860 the residents already enjoyed the privilege of having a local doctor. But it was not until 1867, the year of Confederation, that the original Doctor's House was built. By this time the settlement boasted a lengthy list of skilled craftsmen. In addition to other commercial establishments, there were two hotels, an undertaker and a carriage maker.

The Doctor's House earned its name by being home to a succession of medical men. The original house was gutted in 1974 and then restored to its original architectural design. Continuing the medical tradition, a doctor again practises from this building. The elegant dining and banquet rooms, for which The Doctor's House is so famous, are the result of a major rebuilding and expansion programme which included work on the original Livery.

Afternoon tea at The Doctor's House is served in a pleasingly elegant style. Table decor is perfect. The tea is good and hot. Food, carefully prepared by Executive Chef Timothy K. Mullin, is superb. A selection of delicious tea sandwiches always comes first. Tasty fresh scones, dusted with icing sugar, accompanied by fresh heavy cream and preserves, follow. Then come the fruit tarts and sweets. Sandwich and tart fillings vary with the availability of fresh seasonal produce.

There is a great deal of heritage in this region. Attractions provide something for everyone. Perhaps the most important day of the year is the first Saturday after Labour Day when the Binder Twine Festival is celebrated. The origin of this festival was in the 1890's when the local binder twine dealer began the tradition of providing his customers with a dinner in appreciation of their business. Today, the tradition continues as streets come alive with music and festivities. On a year round basis, the village itself contains a large number of interesting stores.

A visit to the world famous McMichael Art Gallery, which contains the works of great Canadian artists, will delight everyone. And for outdoor fans, the Kortright Centre Conservation Area, containing eighteen kilometres of trails, provides exciting glimpses into Mother Nature's domain.

❄ ❄ ❄

The Great British Emporium
Tricia's Tea Room
NEW DUNDEE, ONTARIO

The small village of New Dundee is famous for two things: the creamery which produces the famous New Dundee Butter and the Emporium. This splendid building, which was recently designated as architecturally significant, has a long and interesting history. It was built by Gottleib Bettschen in 1887, the year of Queen Victoria's Golden Jubilee. In her honour, he named it *The Jubilee Block*. The structure has always been used as a store. Many of the original features, such as counters and bins, are still used today. From 1915 until 1971 the property was owned by Herman Kavelman, who sold a variety of foods and dry goods. In 1971, Mr. and Mrs. William Simpson purchased the property and instituted a tea room in part of the building.

To enter the Emporium is a bit like entering Aladdin's Cave. There is always so much to see. Shelves are stocked with wonderful and unusual goods; and the selection of British sweets always brings back memories of my childhood. I remember the very first time I took tea here. It was a frosty day in the 1970's. The tea was splendid. Outside, snow danced through the air. Inside, damp coats steamed from the heat of an old pot-bellied stove. Somehow both worked towards producing the perfect ambiance for this lovely old Victorian store. What fun it was! And what fun to find a real tea room!

The Simpsons had come from Scotland. As one would expect, most of their tea time treats were standard British fare. Ty-Phoo tea still is the tea of the house. At a time when very few establishments served afternoon tea, devotees of the tea time tradition soon learned that they could always count on a perfect brew as well as generous servings of treats. Consequently, the Emporium built up a large and faithful clientele.

Today the business is owned and operated by Gail Groen and Judy Luft, who continue in much the same way as the Simpsons had. The store still resembles Aladdin's Cave. It is still a magical place full of interesting artifacts and imported goods. Years ago, the tea room was moved to a different part of the building, so the pot bellied stove is no longer a feature. Besides that, there has been little change. As far as the food goes, it is every bit as good as it was twenty years ago. In fact, there are some who declare that the scones at the Emporium are the best in the world.

Teas at the Emporium can be made to order. There is a traditional Scottish Cream Tea with scones, preserves and cream. A crumpet tea consists of two toasted crumpets and tea. Or one may simply order shortbreads and tea. Unlike other tea rooms featured here, the menu at the Emporium does not provide tea sandwiches. However, if you wish to include them in your tea, request them at the time you make a reservation. Lunches are also served and dinner on Friday evenings.

New Dundee is only minutes from any of the splendid attractions offered in Waterloo Region. Museums, galleries, heritage sites, markets, shops, as well as a host of other delightful villages, will enchant any visitor.

❖ ❖ ❖

The Oban Inn
NIAGARA-ON-THE-LAKE, ONTARIO

Niagara-on-the-Lake offers a multitude of pleasures. One of my favourites, in addition to attending splendid theatre productions, is taking afternoon tea at The Oban Inn. White picket fences, shuttered windows, magnificent grounds, and an elegant interior all conspire to give this establishment a wonderful ambiance. The sensation of ages past is so overwhelming that visitors must surely expect to see crinoline-clad women, reclining upon garden seats dotted around the delightful English style gardens which overlook the lake.

The original Inn has been a landmark for one hundred and seventy years. It was originally the home of Captain Duncan Milloy who hailed from Oban, Scotland. Tragically, a devastating fire destroyed this historic building in 1992. The 'new' Oban Inn, rebuilt on the original structure, opened in November 1993 and continues the tradition of gracious service and hospitality.

Afternoon tea at The Oban Inn is served in the stylish conservatory patio. Here, tasteful furnishings set amidst an abundance of decorative plants, offer a comfortable setting. Through picture windows, one can glimpse the colonial splendour which so marks this lovely town. On cold weather days, tea-takers may relax by the fireside in the bar-lounge area. What could be nicer than settling down with a friend or two, toasting your toes and enjoying tea in such lovely sur-roundings?

The tea, beautifully prepared by Chef Tim Erskine, con-sists of a selection of sandwiches—smoked salmon, cucumber, and egg salad are the most popular. Then come buttered scones, served with cream and preserves, followed by delicious homemade pastries. Orange Pekoe is the house tea. Earl Grey, Darjeeling and a selection of other teas are also available.

Niagara-on-the-Lake is a town which offers something for everyone. The most famous attraction is the Shaw Festival, where year after year tremendous theatricals are presented. Those interested in heritage can delight in walking through streets graced with period homes and other structures dating from the very early 1800's. More strenuous hikers can flex their muscles by attempting lengthy treks through magnificent parkland scenery. The town is obviously a shoppers' paradise. Even the most ardent buyer will be kept happy for hours. There are many historical points of interest including muse-ums, and of course, the famous Fort George where daily life in the garrison prior to the War of 1812 is enacted. Further afield, the Niagara Region is packed full of attractions.

❈ ❈ ❈

Royal York Hotel
Royal Tea Room
TORONTO, ONTARIO

Whenever I visit Toronto, I take tea at the Royal York. The fact that this hotel has been involved in serving teas for so many years brings a special quality to the occasion. Merely sitting in the elegant Royal Tea Room is conducive to day-dreaming about the history of this magnificent building.

In 1843 Captain Thomas Dick, a well-known lake-boat captain, built four brick houses on Front Street. Not short of a penny or two, he expanded these buildings into a row. Knox Theological College was housed there until 1853. The building was then turned into the Sword's Hotel. The property went through a number of changes and owners, before Captain Dick returned in 1862 and purchased the property again. He renovated the building, turning it into the stately Queen's Hotel.

A little more than fifty years later, mixed reaction greeted the news that Toronto's beloved Queen's Hotel was to be demolished to make way for the construction of the largest hotel in the British Commonwealth. The Canadian Pacific Railway Company set the wheels in motion and construction began on the sixteen million dollar hotel in 1927. The Royal York opened for business in 1929.

Today, echoes of the past are said to be felt in quiet parts of the hotel. Stories are whispered of a shadowy figure dressed in a full tuxedo wafting through sub-basement vaults. Ghosts or not, since opening, the hotel has attracted famous people from all over the world. Most of the present day British Royal family, as well as royals from other parts of the world, have left their signature in the hotel register. In fact, you never know who you are likely to run into when taking tea at the Royal York. It is a great favourite with a variety of celebrities of stage, screen and television.

Executive Chef George McNeill of the Royal Tea Room. *Royal York Hotel*

In the early days tea was served in the Palm Court, to the strains of the Rex Battle Trio. Today it is served in the truly elegant Royal Tea Room. Here, a real sense of the graciousness of tea time is evident. Tea begins with fresh seasonal berries, followed by one of my favourites, toasted honey crumpets. Then come the dainty sandwiches, all filled with sumptuous concoctions. There are scones served with Devon cream and jam, and, to round things out, a variety of sumptuous finger pastries. Executive Chef, George McNeill, draws from his Scottish background to produce a perfectly wonderful afternoon tea.

A generous supply of Sir Thomas Lipton's brand tea is offered. Loose teas come in English Breakfast, Darjeeling, Russian Earl Grey, Finest Earl Grey, Royal Ceylon and Orange Windsor. There is also a good selection of tea bag blends including black and green teas, decaffeinated, flavoured and herbal teas.

The Royal Tea Room also serve a splendid "Children's Tea." This is geared to accommodate the tastes of children aged five to twelve years of age and includes all the components of the regular afternoon tea, except for sandwiches, which are restricted to egg. In my opinion, taking children to tea at the Royal York is a wonderful treat.

About Cream

The friendly cow, all red and white,
I love with all my heart;
She gives me cream with all her might,
To eat with apple-tart.
ROBERT LOUIS STEVENSON

Many non-farming families kept a cow during the Victorian years. In towns they could be tethered, in villages they were often allowed to graze along the roadside. It made good economic sense. In this way, families were able to provide their own milk, cream and butter. Even so, because producing it involved so much work, clotted cream, or "clouted" cream, as it was sometimes called, was also a great luxury in those days. The following method recommended by Anne Clarke, a noted Canadian cookery expert of the late 1800's, is very similar to that of the famous English cookbook writer, Mrs. Beeton.

Clouted Cream

"In order to obtain this, the milk is suffered to stand in a vessel for twenty-four hours. It is then placed over a stove, or slow fire, and very gradually heated, to an almost simmering state, below the boiling point. When this is accomplished, (the first bubble having appeared), the milk is removed from the fire, and allowed to stand for twenty-four hours more. At the end of this time, the cream will have risen. In this state it is eaten as a luxury; but it is often converted into butter, which is done by stirring it briskly with the hand or a stick. The butter thus made, although more in quantity, is not equal in quality to that procured from the cream which has risen slowly and spontaneously; and in the largest and best dairies, the cream is never clouted, except when intended for the table in that state."[50]

Cream is an important component of afternoon tea. Unfortunately, all too often a good scone is ruined because of using an inferior cream. Over the years I have taken tea in dozens and dozens of tea rooms and have been served everything from squirty imitation stuff in aerosol cans to the most delicious Devon or Cornish cream. Because afternoon teas almost always involve cream, it is useful to know something about the various creams available in our supermarkets. Remember that creams containing less than thirty-five per cent fat will not whip.

Ontario Creams

Half and Half is a light cream containing ten per cent fat. It should not be frozen, nor will it whip. This is a good basic cream for use in cooking. It is ideal for pouring on fruit or cereal, for adding to sauces and for use in coffee and hot chocolate.

Whipping Cream contains thirty-five per cent fat. It will whip to double its original volume and is great for decorating desserts. Add it to trifles for high tea. Spread it between layers of Victoria Sandwich Cakes for afternoon tea, or create masterpieces for any occasion by piping it onto pastries. The viscosity of this cream differs from that of Devonshire, or clotted cream. In a pinch, it can be whipped and slightly sweetened with maple syrup, or other sweetening agent, and served with scones. This cream will freeze for up to two months, but must be whipped first.

Thick Double Cream produced in Ontario has a lower fat content that that produced in Britain. West Hill Dairy produces a forty per cent fat product marketed under the President's Choice label: "Fresh, Thick Double Cream." It can be used direct from the container or whipped to a thicker consistency. It is excellent with scones.

Heavy Cream When restaurants in Ontario speak of "heavy cream," they usually refer to a cream with forty-two per cent fat content. This product is made especially for the restaurant trade and not sold to the general consumer.

Imported Creams

Double Cream is a rich cream containing forty-eight per cent fat. This cream lends itself to cooking. It will pour and it can be whipped. As with whipping cream, it will freeze for up to two months when lightly whipped.

Devonshire Cream is sometimes referred to as extra thick double cream. The fat content is forty-eight per cent —the same as for regular British double cream. This product goes through a process of homogenization which results in a far thicker consistency. Whipping is not necessary since it spoons nicely. This cream is not suitable for freezing. It can be found on the dairy counter in small glass jars with blue labels. It is excellent on scones.

Clotted Cream is the richest of creams. It contains fifty-five per cent fat. It is the ultimate cream for serving with scones. Unfortunately, it is not generally available in North America. Some Canadian tea rooms make a mock clotted cream by adding 1 ounce of sour cream to four ounces of well beaten heavy (40%) cream. One teaspoon of icing sugar is then added and the whole is beaten until very thick. After about six hours the consistency of this cream will change. A little gelatin can be added which may help to bind the mixture together.

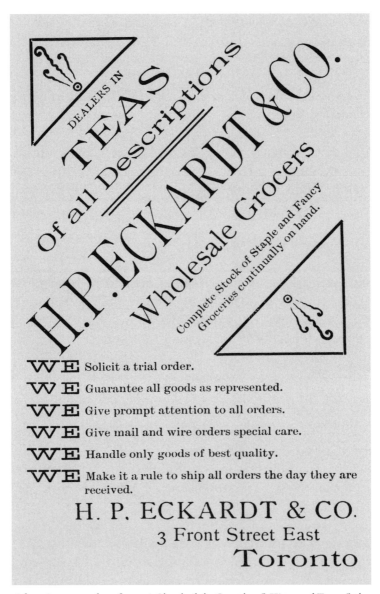

Advertisement taken from *A Sketch of the Growth and History of Tea and the Science of Blending Particularly Adapted to the Canadian Trade. University of Waterloo Archives*

Recipes for Tea Time

--- ❉ ---

Granny's Potted Shrimp

Whenever I taste this marvellous spread, I am immediately transported back to Granny's living-room, where, seated before the fire, we would toast our bread and spread it with this succulent treat. Granny never owned a refrigerator, nor an ice box. She kept her potted shrimp in the coolest part of the pantry where it would last for several days. Fish and seafood came from the coast daily and made popular sandwich fillings.

8 oz. pre-cooked shrimp
1/2 cup clarified butter
1/4 tsp. sea salt
1/4 tsp. Cayenne pepper

Rinse shrimp under running water. Check and remove any specks which were overlooked during the de-veining process. Dry thoroughly. Chop into 1/2 inch size pieces. Place shrimp in a small oven-proof dish. Mix salt, cayenne and 3 ounces of the butter and pour over the shrimps.

Cover with foil and bake 25 minutes at 350°F.

Remove from oven. Drain off the butter and reserve liquid. Pack shrimps into small jar. Any small containers will do but I prefer to use two petite, (125 ml.) glass preserving jars. Pour the cooking liquid back over the shrimps and allow to cool. Seal with 1/4-inch of clarified butter.

Spread generously between pieces of well buttered bread. Trim off the crust and cut into finger sandwiches. It is also excellent spread on hot toast.

❊

Smoked Salmon and Cucumber Sandwiches
MCGREGOR HOUSE

Thin Pumpernickel bread is great for this sandwich.

8 slices of bread
Butter
4 slices of smoked salmon
Thin slices of cucumber
1/4 cup mayonnaise
1 tbsp. minced green onion
1 tbsp. chopped fresh dill
1 1/2 tsp. horseradish
Pinch of pepper

In a small bowl, combine mayonnaise, green onion, dill, horseradish and pepper.

Trim crusts from bread and spread with butter; then with the mayonnaise mixture. Arrange salmon and cucumbers on bread and top with remaining bread. Cut into triangles or squares.

✽

Egg Salad and Watercress Tea Sandwich

ROYAL YORK HOTEL, ROYAL TEA ROOM

Egg Salad Mix:
6 hard boiled eggs, chopped
3 tbsp. mayonnaise
2 green onions, minced
Salt & pepper to taste

Spread mayonnaise on one side of two slices of white sandwich bread. Spread 3 oz. of egg salad mix on one side. Top with sprigs of watercress and cover with remaining slice. Trim crusts and cut into three fingers.

✽

Cucumber and Smoked Salmon Tea Sandwiches

ROYAL YORK HOTEL, ROYAL TEA ROOM

Cucumber
Chopped dill
Atlantic or Pacific smoked salmon, pre-sliced
Bermuda onion, thinly sliced
White and brown sliced bread

Peel and thinly slice cucumber no more than 1/8 of an inch. (If using field cucumbers avoid using seeds.)

Chop the dill.

Using two slices of white and one of brown sandwich bread, spread mayonnaise on one side of each. On top of brown bread lay enough smoked salmon to cover surface. Lay a few slices of onion on top of salmon and top with one slice of white bread. On top of this, lay cut cucumber to cover surface and sprinkle on chopped dill. Top with remaining slice of bread, trim crusts and cut into three fingers.

Shrimp Tea Sandwiches

ROYAL YORK HOTEL, ROYAL TEA ROOM

2 cups baby shrimp (cooked and peeled)
1/4 cup mayonnaise
2 tbsp. chopped fresh parsley
1 tbsp. chopped chives (fresh, dill may be substituted)
Salt & pepper to taste

Mix all ingredients together. Spread mayonnaise on one side of two slices of white bread. Spread approximately 3 oz. of shrimp mix over one slice and top with other. Trim crusts and cut into three fingers.

Chicken Waldorf Sandwiches

MCGREGOR HOUSE

Mix together:
3 cups cooked diced chicken
3/4 cup coarsely chopped walnuts
3/4 cup apples (diced)
1/2 cup raisins
1/2 cup celery
salt and pepper

Combine:
1 cup mayonnaise
1/2 cup sour cream
1/4 cup cider vinegar
1 tbsp. honey

Whisk the dressing and pour over the chicken mixture. Chill for two hours. Assemble sandwiches, trimming off the crust.

❖

Granny's Old Fashioned Cucumber Sandwiches

Cucumber sandwiches are perhaps the most famous of all the afternoon tea sandwiches. They should be prepared immediately prior to serving.

Thinly sliced bread
Thinly sliced English cucumber
1 tbsp. vinegar
Salt and pepper

Peel the cucumber. Slice very thinly and place in a shallow dish. Sprinkle with a little vinegar. Allow to sit for 30 minutes. Drain thoroughly. Sprinkle with salt and pepper. Sandwich cucumber slices between generously buttered bread. Trim crusts and cut into fingers.

❖

Smoked Salmon and Tapanade Finger Sandwich
THE DOCTOR'S HOUSE

2 slices of Bread
Tapanade (see recipe page 100)
Smoked Salmon
Sour Cream

Spread one slice of bread with sour cream. Spread other slice of bread with a thin layer of tapanade. Top with good quality smoked salmon. Put slices together to form sandwich. Cut off crusts and cut remaining sandwich into three equal pieces.

❁

Tapanade

THE DOCTOR'S HOUSE

2 cloves of fresh garlic
2 oz. canned anchovies
1 cup black Italian olives (black throughout)
2 oz. capers
juice from 1/2 lemon
3 oz. olive oil
1 1/2 tsp. Dijon mustard
2 tsp. Brandy

De-salt anchovies by soaking in milk for 10 minutes, then drain.

Puree garlic in food processor. Add anchovies, olives, capers and continue to process until smooth. Add remaining ingredients. Process until you have a smooth paste. Season with fresh pepper and salt if required.

❁

Feta and Garlic Paté

MRS. CARTER'S TEA ROOM

2 cloves garlic, minced
4 anchovy fillets, minced
6 tbsp. butter, softened
10 oz. cream cheese
6 oz. feta
1/4 cup sour cream
1 tbsp. chopped chives
Few drops of Tabasco
Salt & pepper

Combine all in food processor until smooth and creamy.

❉

Aunt Hannah's English Muffins

For at least forty-five years, my brothers and I have debated whether or not one ought to split muffins before toasting them—which is the way I have always preferred them. However, some suggest that only the outsides of the muffin should be toasted. Then they are split and buttered on the soft inside. If I had a penny for every time this topic has been debated around the tea tables of Britain, I'd be a very rich woman.

1 1/2 cups flour
1 tsp. salt
1/3 cup homogenized milk
1/3 cup water
1 tbsp. olive oil
1 tsp. active dry yeast
1/2 tsp. sugar
rice flour

Mix flour and salt together. Set in a warm place.

Heat water, milk and olive oil until tepid. Stir in the sugar and yeast. Leave in a warm place until bubbles appear on the surface.

Make a well in the centre of the flour mixture and pour in the yeast mixture. Stir well, then knead. Cover with a damp cloth and set to rise for about 1 hour, or until double in size.

Punch down and divide into 6 equal pieces. Form into balls, then flatten them down with the palm of your hand. Coat with rice flour, place on a cookie sheet and set them to rise for about 45 minutes.

Lightly coat a heavy fry pan or griddle with oil, and slowly cook the muffins for about 7 minutes on each side. They should become a pale golden brown. Be careful not to overcook them.

Toast and butter generously. Serve warm.

Cooking Victorian Style

The following two recipes are presented exactly as they appeared in publications of the Victorian period. With such directions, our ancestors managed to turn out spectacular dishes. What better testament is needed to their skills?

❖

Victorian Muffins

"These deserve 'extensive circulation.' We have the recipe as a special favour from a lady friend at whose table we have enjoyed some capital specimens..."[51]

> 1 quart milk
> 2 eggs
> Butter
> Flour
> Yeast

To 1 quart of milk, add 2 eggs well beaten, a lump of butter half the size of an egg, and flour enough to make a stiff batter. Stir in half a pint of yeast. Let them stand until perfectly light, and then bake on a griddle, in tin rings made for the purpose.

These are merely strips of tin three-quarters of an inch wide, made into rings from 2 1/2 to 3 inches in diameter, without bottom—the rings simply place on a griddle, and the batter poured in to fill it.

❖

Good Yeast

Grate six good sized potatoes (raw); have ready a gallon of water in which has been well boiled three handfuls of hops; strain through a cloth or sieve, while boiling hot, over the potatoes, stirring until well cooked, or the mixture thickens like starch; add one teacup of sugar, one-half cup of salt; when sufficiently cool, one cup of good yeast. Let it stand until a thick foam rises upon the top. Care must be taken not to bottle too soon, or the bottles may burst.

Use one coffee cup of yeast to six loaves of bread. If kept in a cool place this yeast will last a long time, and housekeepers need not fear having sour bread.[52]

❖

Aunt Hannah's Toasted Teacakes

Tea Cakes are a staple in England. In the north, they appear on just about every tea table. I am told that I began chomping on them long before I had teeth with which to really do them justice. Dunked in warm tea, they kept many a little one quiet for hours. When I was old enough, it was always great fun to toast them over the coal fire. Grandad made an especially long handled toasting fork for doing this.

Tea cakes were also very popular during Victorian times. In grand houses, they would have been served up warm from the kitchen in a muffineer—a dish with a domed lid in which foods such as crumpets, muffins, toast, and tea cakes were kept warm over a lower chamber of hot water.

3/4 cup strong cold tea—strained
1/2 cup currants
1/4 cup mixed peel—chopped
1/2 cup milk
2 tbsp. fine sugar
1 tbsp. dry active yeast
3 cups flour
1 tsp. salt
1/3 cup lard or shortening
1 tsp. of honey and 2 tbsp. milk for glaze
Makes 8

Soak the currants and peel in tea for about 1 hour. Drain, reserving the tea. Add the milk and sugar to the tea and gently heat until tepid. Stir in the yeast, making sure it is thoroughly dissolved.

While the yeast mixture is becoming foamy, stir together the flour and salt. Rub the fat into the flour and then add the fruit, tossing it around so that it is well coated.

Make a well in the centre of the flour and pour the yeast mixture into it. Mix to a soft dough and knead for 10 minutes. Cover and set in a warm place, for about 1 hour - until doubled in size.

Gently knead the dough back to its original size. Divide and roll into 4 inch rounds. Place on cookie sheets, cover with a damp cloth and set to rise again for about 30 minutes.

Heat oven to 375°F and bake for 20 minutes, or until they are a golden brown.

Make the glaze by dissolving honey in warm milk. Brush on the top of the teacakes as they emerge from the oven. Leave to cool. Slice horizontally once or twice, depending upon the thickness. Toast and butter them. Serve hot.

---
*

Scones
ROYAL YORK HOTEL, ROYAL TEA ROOM

2 cups all-purpose flour
1/4 cup granulated sugar
2 tsp. baking powder
1/2 tsp. salt
1/4 cup cold butter
1/2 cup raisins (optional)
2 eggs
1/2 cup milk

Glaze:
1 egg, beaten
Pinch of salt

In a large bowl, combine flour, sugar, baking powder and salt. With pastry blender or fingertips, rub in butter until mixture resembles coarse crumbs. Stir in raisins (optional). Make a well in the centre of flour mixture.

In a small bowl, use a fork to beat eggs and milk until blended. Pour into well. Using a fork, mix with quick, light strokes to make a soft, slightly sticky dough. Press dough into a ball and knead gently on floured surface 10 times.

Pat dough into 3/4-inch thick circle. Cut out, using 2 1/2-inch floured round cutter. Place rounds on a greased baking sheet. Brush tops of scones lightly with egg and salt combination.

Bake in 425°F oven for 15 minutes, or until golden.

Makes 12 scones. Serve with strawberry preserves, cream and tea.

❀

Scones
THE CHÂTEAU LAURIER, ZOÉ'S

14 oz. all purpose flour
4 1/2 oz. of cold butter
2 1/4 oz. of sugar (white)
3/4 oz. double action baking powder
7 oz. of cold homo milk
1 medium egg

Blend all dry ingredients including butter together in a mixer until butter is blended to sandy consistency (pie dough consistency). Add milk & egg and mix until a nice texture (don't overmix). Unfold on a lightly floured table until smooth. (Note—For Sultana raisin scones, mix in 5 oz. of raisins.) Roll out about 1/2-inch thick on a baking sheet. Cut with scone cutter round (2 1/2-inch wide). Egg wash the tops using 1 whole egg blended. Put aside for an hour to allow scones to rise a bit before baking.

Put in the oven at 400° F. Bake until golden brown (10 min.).

Serve warm with Devonshire Cream or fresh strawberry jam.

❖

Granny's Drop Scones

Drop Scones, sometimes referred to as "Scotch Pancakes", are a delightful treat. Children adore them. They are firmer than regular pancakes and can be held in the hand to eat. Granny would serve them hot, spread with her home-made cream cheese. I still eat them this way but with a commercial cream cheese. Drop scones were very popular in Victorian times, served hot and well buttered.

3/4 cup all-purpose flour
1/4 tsp. baking soda
1/2 tsp. cream of tartar
1/4 tsp. salt
1 large egg
1/2 cup milk
2 tsps. caster sugar
Makes about one dozen.

Mix the dry ingredients together.

Beat the egg and stir into the milk. Add sugar to the egg mixture, stirring to dissolve. Gradually add the egg mixture to the dry ingredients stirring until it forms a smooth thick batter.

Heat a heavy griddle, or heavy frying pan, and brush with a little oil. Drop the batter onto the griddle to form drop scones about 3 inches in diameter. Cook on a low heat until bubbles appear on top. Turn them over and cook for the same length of time. Keep hot and serve buttered.

❋

Aunt Hannah's Scones

Scones can be served either warm or cold. Traditionally they are split and spread with butter, heavy cream and preserves. They should be eaten freshly baked. Scones were a weekly feature at our house, and baking up a batch was my Granny's favourite way of using up sour milk. Consequently, we ate many more of them in summer time than we did in winter. Later on, after I was married, I remember staying at Bow Hall near Dufton in West Yorkshire where Sarah Ann Burrows baked goodies for her tea room at Ullswater. After a long morning of hiking in the Vale of Eden, and High Cup Nick, we returned to the Hall with incredible appetites. Upon entering the house, we were greeted by the most wonderful aroma. Five hundred freshly baked scones covered the kitchen table. Sensing our reaction, Sarah Ann immediately brewed us a pot of tea and put together a fabulous tray of goodies. Life was perfect.

2 cups self-raising flour
1/2 tsp. baking soda
1 level tsp. cream of tartar
1/4 tsp. salt
1/3 cup butter
1/2 cup buttermilk or good sour milk

Sift together the flour, baking soda, cream of tartar and salt. Cut in the butter, working until the mixture resembles fine bread crumbs. Pour the milk, all at once, into the mixture. Stir until it binds together into a soft dough.

Roll out the dough until it is 1/2-inch thick. Cut rounds, using a 2 1/2-inch pastry cutter. Place on a baking sheet and bake for 12-15 minutes until they are risen and pale golden brown.

※

Granny's Ginger Treacle Scones

I love ginger at any time of the year. I use it in jams, in sauces for meats, and of course, in cakes, breads, and scones. For a very festive treat, serve these ginger scones piping hot from the oven, smothered in delicious rum butter.

They are also excellent with Devon cream and ginger jam.

1/4 cup of butter
2 cups plain flour
2 tbsp. sugar
Pinch of salt
1 tsp. baking soda
1 tsp. cream of tartar
1 tsp. ground ginger
1/4 cup preserved ginger, finely chopped
1 tbsp. warmed golden syrup or corn syrup
1 egg
Drop of milk

Place the flour, sugar, salt, baking soda, tartar, ground ginger in a mixing bowl. Rub in the butter until the mixture resembles fine bread crumbs.

Warm the syrup *slightly* so that it runs more easily. Beat the egg and mix into the syrup.

Make a well in the middle of the flour mixture. Add egg and syrup and mix lightly until it forms a soft dough. If the mixture is still too dry, add a little milk. Lightly knead in the preserved ginger.

Roll the dough on a floured surface to 1/2-inch thickness. Cut into rounds with a 2 1/2-inch cookie cutter. This amount should make 1 dozen scones. Brush the tops of the scones with a little milk.

Place on a baking sheet and bake at 400°F. for 12 minutes.

❋

Welsh Cakes

MORRISTON TEA ROOM

Welsh cakes make an especially delicious addition to any afternoon tea. They should be well buttered and can be served either hot or cold. Those with an extra sweet tooth may add jam. If well wrapped, they will keep beautifully in the refrigerator for up to six weeks or can be frozen for up to three months. They will also warm nicely in the microwave.

This splendid recipe which has long been popular at the Morriston Tea Room does Marlene Percy's Welsh heritage proud. The tea room, which in my opinion was one of the nicest in the province, was forced to closed its doors at the end of 1996. While Marlene continues to search for a new location, she still operates an afternoon tea business by mail and phone order.

4 cups all-purpose flour
4 tsp. baking powder
1 tsp. salt
1 cup margarine or butter or half of each
1 cup sugar
1 cup currants
4 large eggs

Mix together the flour, baking powder and salt. Blend in the margarine or butter, then the currants. Beat each egg a little, one at a time, then add, a little at a time, to the other ingredients. (This should resemble a pastry dough but a little milk may be necessary to keep it all together.) Divide dough into four balls. Roll out one ball at a time to 1/8-inch thick. Use cookie cutter, whatever size you want, to cut out the cakes.

While doing this, turn on the ungreased griddle to a temperature of about 325-350° F.

Place the cakes on the hot griddle and give them three minutes on each side. They should be a golden brown colour.

❈

Blueberry and Cream Cheese Strata
EAGLEVIEW MANOR

8 slices of bread
3 cups blueberries, fresh or frozen
3 oz. cream cheese
4 well beaten eggs
2 cups milk
1/3 cup white sugar
1 tsp. vanilla
3/4 cup maple syrup
1 tbsp. cornstarch

Butter an 8 inch square baking dish. Cube about 4 slices of bread into the dish. Top with: 1/2 cup blueberries and one 3 oz. package of cream cheese, cubed. Cover with 4 slices of bread, cubed. Add 1/2 cup blueberries.

Mix together: eggs, milk, white sugar and vanilla. Pour over bread mixture. Gently press down. Refrigerate covered for 1 hour, or overnight.

Bake uncovered at 325° F. for about 1 hour.

Serve with Blueberry Maple sauce: 2 cups of blueberries, 3/4 cup of maple syrup and 1 tbsp. of cornstarch. Cook until thickened.

❈

Poppyseed Tea Cake
LANGDON HALL

This is an absolutely marvellous cake. The dough can be fashioned into tiny cookie sized shapes by baking small amounts in molds such as a madeleines. It also looks very attractive when baked in small brioche molds. Remember to adjust the baking time depending upon the size of mold used.

1 kg. all-purpose flour
3 tsp. baking soda
765 grams sugar
675 grams butter
750 grams sour cream
180 grams poppy seeds
13 egg yolks
3 tsp. vanilla

13 egg whites
150 grams sugar

Mix the flour, poppy seeds and baking soda, sift and set aside.

Mix 765 grams of sugar and the butter. Add egg yolks and vanilla and the sour cream. Add the dry ingredients set aside earlier.

Whisk the egg whites and 150 grams of sugar, and incorporate *gently* into the mixture to avoid making the cake too heavy. Divide the cake mixture equally into greased molds.

Bake at 350 degrees Fahrenheit for 35-40 minutes. Let the molds cool on racks.

❋

Cranberry Crumb Squares
THE OBAN INN

3/4 cup softened butter
1/3 cup icing sugar
1 1/2 cups flour
1 pkg. (250 g.) cream cheese, softened
1 can Eagle Brand Sweetened Condensed milk
1/4 cup lemon juice
3 tbsp. brown sugar, divided
2 tbsp. cornstarch
1 can (14 oz.) cranberry sauce (whole)
1/4 cup cold butter
1/3 cup flour
3/4 cup chopped walnuts

Preheat oven to 350° F.

111

Cream together softened butter and icing sugar until light and fluffy. Gradually beat in flour. Press into the bottom of a 13 x 9-inch pan. Bake 15 minutes or until lightly browned.

Reduce oven temperature to 325° F.

In a large bowl, beat cheese until fluffy. Gradually beat in Eagle Brand milk until smooth. Stir in lemon juice. Pour over crust in pan.

In small bowl, combine 1 tbsp. brown sugar and the cornstarch. Mix well. Blend in cranberry sauce. Spoon evenly over cheese mixture.

In a medium bowl, combine remaining brown sugar and 1/3 cup flour. Cut in cold butter with pastry blender until crumbly. Stir in nuts. Sprinkle evenly over cranberry mixture.

Bake 45 to 50 minutes or until bubbly and golden.

❖

Molasses Petite-Gâteau

LANGDON HALL

150 grams all-purpose flour
10 grams baking powder
3 eggs
150 grams sugar
30 grams brown sugar
pinch nutmeg
200 grams melted butter
60 grams molasses

Sift flour and baking powder. Mix eggs, sugar, brown sugar and nutmeg, and then add the sifted flour and baking powder. Add melted butter and molasses. Refrigerate the mixture for 24 hours.

Butter the bottom and sides of a brioche mold or a Madeleine mold with room temperature butter, refrigerate, then butter a second time. Fill 2/3 of the mold with the mixture.

Bake at 325° for 20 minutes.

❖

Best Blueberry Coffee Cake

SILKWEEDS PETTICOAT PARLOUR TEA ROOM

Batter:
4 cups flour
1 1/2 cups sugar
2 tbsp. baking powder
1 tsp. salt
1/2 cup shortening
1 1/2 cups milk
3 eggs
3-4 cups fresh or frozen blueberries (drained)

Topping:
1 cup brown sugar
2/3 cup flour
1/4 cup milk (or less)
1/2 tsp. vanilla

Mix first 7 ingredients. Beat vigorously for 30 seconds. Carefully stir in the blueberries. Spread batter into greased 9x13-inch pan.

Sprinkle topping over batter and bake at 350° F. 40 - 45 mins.

When cool, ice with thin powdered sugar glaze.

❖

Granny's Victoria Sandwich Cake

1 cup butter
1 cup fine caster sugar
3 large eggs
2 cups self-raising flour
Pinch of salt
1/4 tsp. lemon juice

Cream the butter and sugar together until very light and fluffy. Add well beaten eggs a drop at a time until well mixed. Sift together flour and salt and gently fold into the butter mixture. Add lemon juice.

Divide batter between two lined and greased 8 x 1 1/2-inch cake tins.

Bake at 375° F. 20 - 25 minutes.

Remove from oven when centre is springy to touch. Allow to cool for 5 minutes and then turn out of cake pans onto a wire cooling rack.

When cold, sandwich together using strawberry jam. Sprinkle icing sugar lightly over the top.

Apple Almond Pound Cake

THE CHÂTEAU LAURIER, ZOÉ'S

500 grams butter
500 grams sugar
400 grams ground white almonds
500 grams flour
300 grams peeled grated apples
150 grams orange or lemon peel (optional)
12 eggs
10 grams baking powder
1 orange rind
grated ginger
salt

Yield 2 cakes–8 x 3 x 3 inch

Cream butter and sugar. Add eggs one by one. Add grated peeled apples, orange peel, ginger and salt.

Mix flour, baking powder and white ground almonds together. Mix in dry ingredients, do not overmix.

Fill in pan, lined with parchment paper or buttered.

Bake at 350° F. To test, insert a small knife.

❖

Granny's Dundee Cake

This cake needs to ripen for several weeks. Brush periodically with whiskey.

1 cup currants
1 cup raisins
1/2 cup sultanas
1/2 cup glacé cherries
1/2 cup candied peel
1/4 cup whiskey
2 cups flour
1 tsp. baking powder
3/4 cup butter
3/4 cup soft brown sugar
3 eggs
2 tbsp. ground almonds
Grated zest of 1 orange & 1 lemon
1/3 cup whole blanched almonds for decorating

Soak dried fruit overnight in 1/4 cup of whiskey.

Beat butter and sugar. Whisk eggs and slowly add to butter mixture. Carefully fold in the flour and baking powder. (Mixture should be of a soft dropping consistency. If necessary, add a little milk.) Carefully fold in ground almonds, fruits, peel and rinds. Spoon mixture into greased and floured 8-inch round cake pan. If desired, decorate the top by *lightly* pressing blanched almonds into the batter.

Bake 2–2 1/2 hours at 325°F. in centre of oven.

When cool, feed the cake by brushing all over with whiskey.

Wrap well in cheese cloth, then wax paper.

--- ❈ ---

Farmhouse Tea Cake

QUEENSTON HEIGHTS RESTAURANT

1/2 lb. butter
Grated zest of 1 lemon and 1 orange
1 cup fine sugar
1/2 cup raisins
1 cup chopped dry figs
1 cup currants
2/3 cup candied mixed peel
2 1/2 cups unbleached flour
1 1/2 tsp. baking powder
pinch of salt
1/2 cup ground almonds
4 eggs
2 tbsp. dark rum
2 tbsp. milk
30 blanched almonds.

Preheat oven to 325° F.

Lightly grease a 9 x 5 x 3-inch loaf pan and line it with waxed paper.

Cream butter and sugar and citrus zest until pale and fluffy.

Place raisins, figs, currants and mixed peel in a bowl.

Sift flour, baking powder and salt together well. Add 1/2 cup of flour mixture to the dried fruit mixture and mix well.

Add ground almonds to the sugar and butter mixture. Add the eggs, one at a time, beating well after each addition. Gradually fold in remaining flour, rum and fruit mixture. Spoon mixture into loaf pan.

Dip the blanched almonds into the milk and arrange on top of cake.

Bake 2 - 2 1/2 hours.

✿

Fruit Tart
THE DOCTOR'S HOUSE

Old Fashioned Lemon Tart Filling:
1 1/4 cups granulated sugar
1/3 cup cornstarch
1/4 tsp. salt
1 1/4 cup cold water
1/2 cup lemon juice (5-6 lemons)
3 large egg yolks (beaten)
2 tsp. lemon zest
2 tbsp. sweet butter

Add first six ingredients to pan. Stir well. Cook on medium heat stirring slowly until mixture begins to boil and thicken. Lower temperature and continue to cook for one minute. Remove from heat. Add lemon zest and butter.
Makes enough filling for 18 to 24 tarts depending on size.

Fruit Tart Assembly: Make Sweet Paste according to directions on page 119. Bake tart shells. Make lemon filling and pour the warm filling into tart shells. Let cool. Garnish tops with seasonal fruit. Mango, strawberries, kiwi, raspberries, peaches, papaya, orange segments, lychees, blueberries or blackberries.

✿

Lemon Cheese Bar
THE OBAN INN

1 Duncan Hines yellow cake mix
1 - 8 oz. pkg. cream cheese, softened
1/3 cup sugar
1 teaspoon lemon juice
2 eggs
1/3 cup oil

Mix dry cake mix, 1 egg and oil until crumbly. Reserve 1 cup.

Pat remaining mixture lightly in an ungreased 13 x 9 x 2-inch pan.

Bake 15 minutes at 350° F.

Beat cheese, sugar, lemon juice and 1 egg until light and smooth. Spread over baked layer. Sprinkle with reserved crumb mixture. Bake 15 minutes longer.

Cool. Cut into bars.

❄

Coffee Frangipan Cake
THE CHÂTEAU LAURIER, ZOÉ'S

4 oz. butter
4 oz. sugar
4 oz. white ground almonds
2 eggs
1 1/2 oz. flour
Salt
Instant coffee to taste

Yield
One 10" Tart

Line a flan shell with Sweet Paste (See page 119). Cover lightly with apricot jam.

Cream butter and sugar. Add eggs and salt. Mix coffee with a little water and add it to butter mix.

Mix flour and almonds. Fold into the butter mix. Do not overmix. Fill in a pre-lined sweet paste shell. Sprinkle with white sliced almonds and bake at 340° F.

❋

Sweet Paste
THE DOCTOR'S HOUSE

2/3 cup granulated sugar
1 cup sweet butter (room temperature)
3 1/4 cups pastry flour
1 whole egg (large)
1/8 cup whole milk
1 tsp. Salt

Cream sugar and butter. Mix egg, milk and salt together. Add flour in two stages to sugar butter mixture, alternating with egg mixture. Mix to homogeneous mass. Do not over-mix as this will develop the gluten (becomes elastic and tough). Let sweet paste rest for one hour before using.

❋

Chocolate Slice
THE OBAN INN

1/2 cup butter
1/2 cup brown sugar
3/4 cup flour (bread)
2 tbsp. cocoa
1 tsp. vanilla
1 egg
1/2 can Eagle Brand Sweetened Condensed Milk
2 cups coconut

Cream butter, sugar and cocoa. Beat in egg. Add vanilla and flour. Mix well and pat into a greased 8-inch pan.

Take 1/2 can of Eagle Brand milk and add coconut. Spread over chocolate mixture. Bake 20 to 25 minutes at 350° F.

Ice with chocolate icing.

Shortbread

THE EMPORIUM

This wonderful shortbread is served daily at the Emporium. Because the recipe is so rich, the shortbread does not lend itself to cutting into fancy shapes with cookie cutters. It is best cut into fingers.

1 pound salted butter
1 pound unsalted butter
2 cups white sugar
2 egg yolks
8 cups of all purpose flour

Let butter soften to room temperature. Cream butter well in basin. Cream in egg yolks and sugar. Add flour in stainless steel basin and work in with paddle as well as you can. Knead until a stiffish workable ball of dough.

Working with half of dough, roll to between 1/4 and 1/2-inch thickness. Cut into fingers about 3/4 x 1 inch.

Put on ungreased cookie sheet, prick 3-4 times with a fork.

Bake at 350° F. for 18 minutes. Turn pan and bake a further 4-5 minutes until set and faintly gold tinged.

Cool on pan and store in cookie tin between layers of waxed paper.

Lemon Curd

EAGLEVIEW MANOR

Microwave 1/2 cup of butter. Add 1 cup of white sugar, 1/2 cup of lemon juice, and 3 large eggs, well beaten.

Cook until thick, stirring occasionally.

❋

Lemon Blossom Cookies
MRS. CARTER'S TEA ROOM

2 cups butter
1 1/2 cups icing sugar
1/3 cup lemon juice
4 cups all-purpose flour
2 1/4 cups finely chopped nuts

Beat butter and icing sugar in mixer until light and fluffy. Add lemon juice and mix well. Gradually add flour, mixing until smooth. Chill for two hours.

Shape into 1 inch balls. Roll in nuts. Place 1 inch apart on lined baking sheets. Press thumb in centre of each ball. Fill with jam.

Bake at 350°F for 12 to 15 minutes or until lightly browned. Makes approximately 2 dozen.

❋

Granny's Lemon Cheese

Lemon Cheese, or, Lemon Curd, as it is called in North America, is always a very popular item at our house. We use it on all manner of things. It is wonderful in tarts, but I love it best on scones. If stored in a cool place, Lemon Cheese will keep for several months.

1/2 cup fine caster or fruit sugar
Zest and juice from one large or 2 small lemons
3 large eggs
1/3 cup unsalted butter

Beat eggs. Stir in lemon juice, sugar and lemon zest. Cut up butter and add to lemon mixture. Place in a bowl over gently simmering water. Stir frequently.

Cook for about thirty minutes. The lemon cheese is done when it nicely coats the back of a spoon.

Place in small sterilized jars and seal.

❀

Granny's Rum Butter

Rum butter, which my family only used at Christmas time, is a very festive food in England. It is one of those ancient concoctions surrounded by a great deal of tradition. In some parts of the country, pregnant women prepared this dish during their sixth month of pregnancy. It was then safely tucked away in a cool place until baby arrived. The rum butter was then served up to well-wishers on biscuits. I always make this recipe at the end of October along with Christmas items which need to mellow. It is marvellous served on ginger scones and on hot mince pies.

1/2 cup unsalted butter
1 firmly packed cup of dark brown sugar
1/2 level tsp. grated nutmeg
1/4 cup rum
1/3 cup unsalted butter

Soften the butter, being sure not to let it melt. Beat in the sugar and mix until very light and fluffy. Stir in the grated nutmeg, mixing well so that the flavour is evenly dispersed. Gradually stir in the rum, beating thoroughly.

Press the rum butter into small containers and chill.

Some closing thoughts...

Most people have their own special recipes for preserves. My father drove to market weekly often returning with splendid assortments of fruits which Mother turned into jams and jellies. A favourite at our house was greengage plum jam. Granny grew gooseberries and they, too, were highly prized. For those who are not inclined towards making their own preserves, excellent varieties of interesting jams and jellies are available in specialty shops. In addition to sweet jams, it is important, when planning an afternoon tea, not to overlook the usefulness of savoury spreads. Marmite, though perhaps an acquired taste, makes a delicious treat on toast fingers. Pepper jelly and cream cheese is also a wonderful combination. Cheese goes particularly well with Marlene Percy's Welsh Cakes. The combinations are endless! Be creative.

The most wonderful thing about afternoon tea is the wide scope it offers. For very little cost, a sumptuous and impressive spread can be whipped up. Tea time can be an incredibly elegant affair prepared with a great deal of fussing. It can also be a simple and relaxing occasion. Whichever you choose, it is simply one of the most perfect ways of entertaining.

Suppliers

General Information about Tea

Tea Council of Canada
301-885 Don Mills Road
Don Mills ON M3C 1V9
Newsletters and Tea *Health Letter* bulletin available on request.

Tea Suppliers - mail/phone order

C.J. Distributors, (India Teas)
21 Calverley Trail,
Scarborough ON M1C 3R3
416-283-8465
Indian "Imperial Tea" range.
Approved by the Tea Board of
India.

Cooke's Old World Shop Ltd.
61 Brock Street
P.O. Box 66
Kingston ON K7L 4V6
613-548-7721
Toll Free 1-800-576-5866
Fax 613-548-3449
Complete line of Twining,
Jacksons of Piccadilly, Bigelow,
Celestial Seasonings, and the spe-
cial house blend: Garden Island.

McKee's Tea & Coffee House
Bramalea City Centre
25 Peel Centre Drive
Brampton ON L6T 3R5
905-791-5665

Specialty teas and accessories.
Will blend private labels.

Morriston Tea Room
Marleene Percy
P.O. Box 84
Morriston ON N0B 2C0
519-823-0564
Mail order Tea and accessories.
Tea time treats - baking etc.

Murchies Tea & Coffee Ltd.
5580 Parkwood Way
Richmond B.C. V6V 2M4
1-604-231-7500
Toll Free 1-800-663-0400
Catalogue and *Murchie Times*
newsletter upon request.

Say Tea
2362 Bloor Street West
Toronto ON M6S 1P3
416-766-5425
Metropolitan Tea Co and "Say
Tea" label.

The China Tea Co,
174 Johnston Road, G/F
G.P.O. Box 5680
Hong Kong

The Herb Garden
2055 Worthington Drive
Oakville ON L6L 1E2
905-847-0266
Mail order / phone order
Direct Sales:
The Picket Fence
Fergus Market
Queen Street E. (Hwy #6)
Fergus ON
Saturday and Sundays

The Tea Party
119 York Street
Ottawa ON K1N 5T4
613-562-0352
Mail Order

Whittard of Chelsea
73 Northcote Road
London SW11 6PJ
England
Catalogue / Mail Order.

Victoria Gallery and Tea
108 Queen Street
Niagara -on-the-Lake ON
L0S 1J0
905-468-5707

Tea Pots and Accessories
Direct sales only
Mad River Tea House
Mill Street, Creemore ON
705-466-3526
Tea and accessories
Over 300 different tea pots
Closed Dec 24–April 15

Cast Iron Griddle Irons:
Available at Canadian Tire Stores

Selected Tea Rooms in Ontario

Eagleview Manor
Reservations required
Address: 178 Widder St. E.
St. Marys ON N4X 1A8
519-284-1811

Owners: Bob and Pat Young

Hours: Nanny's Tea room open: 1:00 p.m.– 6:00 p.m.
Cost: Afternoon tea $10.00. Discount for groups of 6 or more.
Wheelchairs: One small entrance step.
Smoke Free.

How to get there: From Toronto take 401 to Highway 7/8. Exit at Interchange #278 near Kitchener. Take highway 7/8 west to Stratford, then 7/19. Turn north for St. Marys about 16 km. west of Stratford. At the Town Hall, located at the corner of Queen and Church, travel north two blocks to Widder. Turn right, Eagleview Manor is on the right hand side.

Langdon Hall Country House Hotel
Reservations required
Address: R. R. 33
Cambridge ON N3H 4R8
519-740-2100
Fax: 519-740-8161

Manager: Martin Stitt
Chef: Louise Duhamel

Afternoon Tea is served: 3.00 p.m.–5.00 p.m.
Cost: $13.75 – $27.00
Wheelchair accessible.

How to get there: Travelling east from London, or west from Toronto, take Highway 401 to Exit 275 Homer Watson Blvd. (Exit 275 is situated west of Highway 8 to Kitchener and Waterloo.) Travel south on Fountain

Street/Homer Watson Blvd. to Blair Road, which will be the second road on your right, and follow the signpost to Blair. Go through the village of Blair to Langdon Road, the second on your right. Then, after approximately 100 feet, turn at the first driveway on the left (partially hidden by trees) and follow the lane approximately 1/2 km. up to Langdon Hall.

McGregor House
Reservations recommended
Address: 123 Leeder Lane
Southampton ON N0H 2L0
519-797-1702

Owners: Jan and Anne Riddall

Hours: Wednesday–Saturday 11 a.m.–5 p.m.
Sunday 12 noon–5 p.m.
Winter months–closed Sundays
Cost: Cream Tea $3.95
Afternoon tea for two $14.95
Children's Tea $2.95
Wheelchair: One step
Smoke Free

How to get there: Southhampton is on Lake Huron, to the west of Owen Sound. Approaching Southampton from Highway 21, turn left at the stop light on to High Street. Make a left turn on to Grosvenor Street, then right on to Leeder Lane.

Mrs. Carter's
Reservations not essential
Mrs. Carter's Bakery-Restaurant-Tea Room
116 Downie Street
Stratford ON
519-271-9200

Owner: Laura Carter

Hours: Tea served from 3:00–5:00
Cost for tea: $3.95–$8.95
Wheelchair: Two small steps to enter the building.

How to get there: Highway 7/8, from the direction of Kitchener, becomes Ontario Street, Stratford. Continue along Ontario Street until into the downtown section. Make a left turn on to Downie Street. Mrs. Carter's is on the right hand side.

Queenston Heights Restaurant
Reservations required
14184 Niagara Parkway
Mailing Address: c/o Niagara Parks Commission
P.O. Box 150 Niagara Falls ON L2E 6T2
905-262-4274

Manager: Carol Muscato
Chef: Herbert Baur

Hours: Afternoon tea is served from 3:00–5:00
May 3rd–June 28, Saturday & Sunday only
June 29–September 1, Daily
September 6–October 19, Saturday & Sunday only
Cost for tea: $9.25
Wheelchair accessible

How to get there: Take the Queen Elizabeth Way past St. Catharines. Exit at Interchange #37 on to Highway 405 to Queenston. The Brock monument atop Queenston Heights is adjacent to the restaurant and provides a suitable landmark.

Silkweeds Petticoat Parlour Victorian Tea Room
Reservations required for the full afternoon tea.
Address: 23 Main Street South
St. George ON N0E 1N0
519-448-3285

Owners: Holly Woelfle and Jackie Entichnapp

Closed: Monday except for Holiday Mondays
Hours: 1:00 p.m.–4:30 p.m.
Cost: Afternoon Tea $10.95, Cream Tea $5.95
Private functions can be arranged
Wheelchair accessible

How to get there: From Toronto take Highway 5 west. Make a right turn in to St. George about 34 km west of Waterdown, a few kilometres east of Highway 24. From Cambridge, take Highway 24 south to Highway 5. Turn left into St. George. The tea room is at 23 Main Street South, St.

George, located in the block across from the South Dumfries Township Hall.

The Château Laurier

Zoé's
Reservations recommended
Address: 1 Rideau Street
Ottawa ON K1N 8S7
613-241-1414
Toll Free: 1-800-441-1414
Fax: 613-562-7030

Executive Chef Patissier: Ernst Frehner

Hours: 3:00 p.m.–5:30 p.m. Mon–Sat
4:00 p.m.–5:30 p.m. Sun.
Cost: $13.50
Wheelchair accessible.

How to get there: The Château Laurier is located in downtown Ottawa, immediately adjacent to the Rideau waterway and the Parliament Buildings.

The Doctor's House

Reservations recommended
Address: 21 Nashville Road
Kleinburg ON L0J 1C0
905-893-1615
Fax: 905-893-0660

Manager: Pat Boutette
Executive Chef: Timothy K. Mullin

Hours: 3:00 p.m.–5:00 p.m. Mon.–Sat.
4:00 p.m.–5:00 p.m. Sun.
Cost: Afternoon Tea $10.00
Wheelchair accessible

How to get there: From Toronto take Highway 400 north to exit #35. Travel west on Highway 25 to Kleinburg. Alternatively, Kleinburg is just east of Highway 27 approximately 10 km. north of Pearson International Airport. Find The Doctor's House on Nashville Road near Islington Avenue. The white picket fence surrounding the property will help to identify this establishment.

The Great British Emporium

Reservations–Only required for groups
Address: 169 Front Street
New Dundee ON N0B 2E0
519-696-2223

Owners: Gail Groen and Judy Luft

Hours: 10:00 a.m.–5:00 p.m. (Closed Monday)
Cost: Cream Tea $3.95
Crumpet Tea $3.25
Wheelchair accessible–no special washroom.

How to get there: From Toronto, take Highway 401 to Highway 7/8 near Kitchener (exit at Interchange #278). Take 7/8 west towards Stratford. Travel south on road #12 soon after leaving the builtup area of Kitchener, for about 10 km in to the village. Turn left on to Front Street at the Creamery. From Stratford, travel east on Highway 7/8 to Waterloo Road 12. Turn right to New Dundee.

The Oban Inn

Reservations recommended
Address: 160 Front Street
Post Office Box 94
Niagara-on-the-Lake
ON L0S 1J0
905-468-2165
Fax: 905-468-4165

General Manager: Gary Burroughs
Chef: Tim Erskine

Hours: 3:00 p.m.–5:00 p.m. except on Saturdays
Cost: Afternoon Tea–$7.50
Wheelchair accessible

How to get there: Take the Queen Elizabeth Way until south of St. Catharines. Exit at Interchange #38, Highway 55. Travel approximately 13 km to Niagara-on-the-Lake. The Oban Inn is located at the corner of Front and Gate Streets, overlooking Lake Ontario.

The Royal Tea Room

Reservations recommended
Address: Royal York Hotel
100 Front Street West
Toronto ON M5J 1E3
416-368-2511
Fax: 416-860-5098

Supervisor: Kerry Shepherd
Executive Chef: George McNeill

Hours: Tea is served from 12 noon until 5.00 p.m. Mon.–Fri.
2:00 p.m.–5:00 p.m. Sat. and Sun.
Cost: Afternoon Tea $13.50
Children's Tea $6.75
Wheelchair accessible.

How to get there: The Royal York Hotel is in the heart of downtown Toronto, across from Union Station, at the corner of Front and York Streets.

Notes

1   *The Story of Tea*. (Toronto, The Tea Bureau, 1939).

2   *The Illustrated Pepys: Extracts from the Diary*, selected and edited by Robert Latham. (London, Bell and Hyman Limited, 1978), p. 148.

3   Frederick Dane and R. S. McIndoe, *A Sketch of the Growth and History of Tea and the Science of Blending Particularly Adapted to the Canadian Trade*. (Toronto, Department of Agriculture, 1891), p. 12.

4   *Elmira Signet*, 15 December, 1904.

5   Johnson quote: Review in the 'Literary Magazine,' vol. ii. No. xiii. 1757.

6   Hudson's Bay Company Archives, A. 24/2, p. 76.

7   Ibid, p. 130.

8   Frederick Dane and R. S. McIndoe, *A Sketch of the Growth and History of Tea and the Science of Blending Particularly Adapted to the Canadian Trade*. (Toronto, Department of Agriculture, 1891), p. 16.

9   T.G. Ridout, 4 Mile Creek, September 4, 1813 (Courtesy, Richard Feltoe, Archives on War of 1812.

10   Charles Francis Hall, *Artic Researches and Life Among the Esquimaux*. (New York, Harpers and Brothers, 1866), pp 161-162.

11   *Mrs. Simcoe's Diary*, Edited by Mary Quayle Innis. (Toronto, MacMillan of Canada, 1965).

12   *A Gentlewoman in Upper Canada: The Journals of Anne Langton*. Edited by H. H. Langton. (Toronto, Irwin Publishing, 1950), p. 35.

13   Haight, Canniff, *Country Life in Canada*. (Toronto, Hunter, Rose & Co., 1885). Reprinted by Mika Publishing Co., Belleville, Ontario, 1977.

14   Courtesy Lipton Tea Company

15   Robina and Kathleen MacFarlane Lizars, *In the Days of the Canada Company: The Story of The Settlement of the Huron Tract and a View of the Social Life of the Period*. (Toronto, William Briggs, 1892), p. 182.

16   Susanna Moodie *Life in the Clearings versus the Bush*. (New Canadian Library: unabridged reprint of 1st edition, 1853; 1899), Chapter 18, p. 311.

17   Copied from a typed card at The Fairfield White House, near Amherstview, where staff attributed these instructions to Catherine (Geddes) Macaulay.

18   Diary of Louise J. Breithaupt, November 21, 1867.

19   Ibid, November 22, 1867.

20   Ibid, August 16, 1884.

21 Frances Hoffman and Ryan Taylor, *Much To Be Done: Private Life in Ontario From Victorian Diaries.*(Toronto, Natural Heritage/Natural History, 1996), p. 155.

22 M. Loane, *The Queen's Poor: Life as they Find it in Country and Town.* (London, Edward Arnold, 1910), p. 119.

23 Robin Harris and Terry Harris, *The Eldon House Diaries: Five Women's Views of the 19th Century* (Toronto, The Champlain Society, 1944), p. 433.

24 *The Home Cook Book.*(Toronto, Rose Publishing Co., 1877), p. 34.

25 *Manitoba Morning Free Press*, (Winnipeg), 11 October 1895.

26 Diary of Frances Gay Simpson, January 29, 1881.

27 T. Eaton and Company, Fall and Winter Catalogue, September 1890, p. 50.

28 Ibid, Fall and Winter Catalogue, 1918-1919, p. 530.

29 *The New Galt Cookbook*. (Toronto, McLeod & Allen, 1898), p. 264.

30 Ibid, p. 262.

31 *The Ladies' Home Journal*, (Toronto), May 1896.

32 Ibid, February, 1890.

33 *Kingston Whig Standard*, December 14, 1938, p. 6.

34 Diary of Louis J. Breithaupt, 11 October 1892.

35 Ibid, 30 May 1892.

36 Diary of Florence Grace Clement, 28 January 1928.

37 James Boswell, *Tour to the Hebrides*, 1773.

38 *The New Galt Cookbook*. (Toronto, McLeod & Allen, 1898), p. 375.

39 *The History of Twining Blends According to Sam Twining (9th generation Twining)*, Ref.: 1/SHG/1/194. Press Release.

40 *The Berlin Daily Telegraph*, 12 April 1899, p. 2

41 Linda Hull Larned, *The Hostess of To-Day*. (New York, Charles Scribner's Sons, 1899).

42 *The Finchley Manual of Industry No .111: Female Servant Manual.* (London, Joseph Masters, 1867).

43 Thomas Lymer Papers, Archives of Ontario, MU 4573-F1035.

44 Diary of Louis J. Breithaupt, 15 January 1900.

45 Ibid, 26 December 1911.

46 Diary of Catherine Olive Breithaupt, 2 January 1914.

47 Ibid, 11 February 1914.

48 Ibid, 2 January, 1914.

49 Ibid, 16 May 1914.

50 Anne Clarke, *The Dominion Cookbook*. (Toronto, McLeod & Allen, 1899), p. 244.

51 *The Spirit of the Age*, (Barrie, Ontario),23 February 1859.

52 *The Canadian Home Cookbook*. (Toronto, Hunter, Rose and Company, 1877), p. 268.

Source Notes to Poems

Photo reference numbers

Selected Bibliography

A Gentlewoman in Upper Canada: The Journals of Anne Langton. Edited by H. H. Langton. (Toronto, Irwin Publishing, 1950).

Haight Canniff, *Country Life in Canada.* (Toronto, Hunter, Rose & Co. 1885). Reprinted by Mika Publishing Co, Belleville, Ontario, 1977.

Clark, Ann, *The Dominion Cookbook.* (Toronto, McLeod & Allen, 1899).

Dane, Frederick and McIndoe, R. S. , *A Sketch of the Growth and History of Tea and the Science of Blending Particularly Adapted to the Canadian Trade.* (Toronto, Department of Agriculture, 1891). University of Waterloo Archives.

Breithaupt, Diary of Catherine Olive, (Breithaupt Hewetson-Clarke Collection), University of Waterloo Archives.

Clement, Diary of Florence Grace, (Clement Bowlby Papers), University of Waterloo Archives.

Breithaupt, Diary of Louis J., (Breithaupt Hewetson-Clarke Collection), University of Waterloo Archives. Translated by Jane Forgay through the assistance of a grant from the Waterloo Regional Heritage Foundation.

Simpson, Diary of Frances Gay, National Archives of Canada, MG4 K48.

Hall, Charles Francis, *Artic Researches and Life Among the Esquimaux,* (New York, Harpers and Brothers, 1866).

Harris, Robin and Harris, Terry, *The Eldon House Diaries: Five Women's Views of the 19th Century,* (Toronto, The Champlain Society, 1944).

Hoffman, Frances and Taylor, Ryan, *Much To Be Done: Private Life in Ontario from Victorian Diaries.* (Toronto, Natural Heritage / Natural History Inc., 1996).

Larned, Linda Hull, *The Hostess of To-Day*. (New York, Charles Scribner's Sons, 1899).

Loane, M., *The Queen's Poor: Life as they Find it in Country and Town*. (London, Edward Arnold, 1910).

Mrs. Simcoe's Diary. Edited by Mary Quayle Innis. (Toronto, MacMillan of Canada, 1965).

Pain, Barry, *Playthings and Parodies*, (London, Cassell & Company, Limited, 1892).

The Berlin Daily Telegraph, (Berlin, Ontario).

The Elmira Signet. (Elmira, Ontario).

The Finchley Manual of Industry no 111: Female Servant Manual. (London, Joseph Masters, 1867). J.E.G. Curran Papers, National Archives of Canada, MG C85 Vol. 4.

The Home Cook Book. (Toronto, Rose Publishing Co., 1877).

The Illustrated Pepys: Extracts from the Diary, Selected and Edited by Robert Latham. (London, Bell and Hyman Limited, 1978).

The Ladies' Home Journal. (Toronto, Ontario).

The Manitoba Morning Free Press. (Winnipeg, Manitoba).

The New Galt Cookbook. (Toronto, McLeod & Allen, 1898).

The Spirit of the Age. (Barrie, Ontario).

The Story of Tea. (Toronto, The Tea Bureau, 1939).

The Thomas Lymer Papers, Archives of Ontario, MU 4573-F1035.

The Victoria Colonist, (Victoria, British Columbia).

Index

About the Author

Frances Hoffman was born and raised in the north of England. Some of her female relatives, particularly a great aunt, encouraged her interest in social history. Whether in Lancashire towns, isolated pockets of the Yorkshire Moors, or Great Aunt Hannah's 350 year old farmhouse nestled in the Derbyshire Pennines, the tea table and the tradition of tea were always very much part of her family life.

She came to Canada in 1966 and lives in a log house on the banks of the Grand River in the heart of Mennonite country near Waterloo, Ontario. It was while entertaining Old Order Mennonite neighbours at afternoon tea that her previous publication, *Much To Be Done: Life in Ontario from Victorian Diaries*, (co-authored with Ryan Taylor) was conceived.

Frances Hoffman is employed as an oral historian by the Kitchener Public Library. She presently serves as Chair of the Waterloo-Wellington Branch of the Ontario Genealogical Society, Secretary to the Maryhill Historical Society, and is a former board member of the Waterloo Regional Heritage Foundation.